International Diabetes Center

Diabetes Care Made Easy

A Simple Step-By-Step Guide For Controlling Your Diabetes

Allison Nemanic, RN, BA • Gretchen Kauth RD, CDE
Marion J. Franz, MS, RD, CDE
Illustrated by Jan Westberg

Copyright © 1992 by the International Diabetes Center.
Park Nicollet Medical Foundation.

All rights reserved. Except for brief passages used for review purposes, no part of this publication may be reproduced, stored in a retrieval system or transmitted, in any form or by any means, electronic, photocopying, recording, or otherwise, without the prior written permission of CHRONIMED Publishing.

Library of Congress Cataloging-in-Publication Data

Nemanic, Allison.
    Diabetes care made easy: a simple step-by-step guide for controlling your diabetes/Allison Nemanic, Gretchen Kauth, Marion Franz.
        p.   cm.
    Includes bibliographical references and index.
    Summary: Describes how persons with diabetes can care for themselves, discussing how to take insulin, what foods to eat or avoid, and what exercises to do.
    ISBN 1-56561-013-X: $9.95
    1. Diabetes in children – Juvenile literature.
    [1. Diabetes]
I. Kauth, Gretchen. II. Franz, Marion J. III. Title.
RJ420.D5N46   1992   92-11193
618-92'462 – dc20   CIP
                                                        AC

10 9 8 7 6 5 4 3 2

Special thanks to:
Jan Westberg, Designer/Illustrator
May Typography, Type and Keyline
The Staff of the IDC for suggestions, review and support.

Funded by a grant from the Gamble-Skogmo Foundation.

Melanie Brüngel-Dittrich

Speech Presentation in the British and German Press

Frankfurt am Main, Berlin, Bern, Bruxelles, New York, Oxford, Wien, 2006.
266 pp., 37 tab., 47 graf.
European University Studies: Series 21, Linguistics. Vol. 297
ISBN 3-631-54948-2 / US-ISBN 0-8204-9858-0 · pb. € 45.50*

This book is a comparative linguistic study analysing the phenomenon of speech presentation or *Redewiedergabe* in a corpus of British and German newspaper articles. By applying a modified speech presentation model to a corpus of 143 articles – originally, the prototype had been designed for the analysis of English literary texts – the author shows that it is possible to examine journalistic texts stylistically and to compare texts written in different languages. The analysis, divided into a qualitative and a quantitative part, reveals that the genre of a text or paper influences the use of speech presentation to a high extent. Differences between the German and English texts in terms of language structure and also newspaper culture are highlighted, involving an examination of the use of reporting verbs, the subjunctive and *berichtete Rede* in the German articles.

Contents: Speech presentation – models for the English and the German language · Newspapers on the Internet · Qualitative and quantitative analysis of speech presentation in British and German newspaper articles · Reporting verbs in British and German newspapers articles · Comparison of results with existing studies and theories · The use of the subjunctive in German news texts · *Berichtete Rede* · Speech presentation in headlines

Insulin helps your body use the sugar made from the food you eat. Insulin is made in the pancreas.

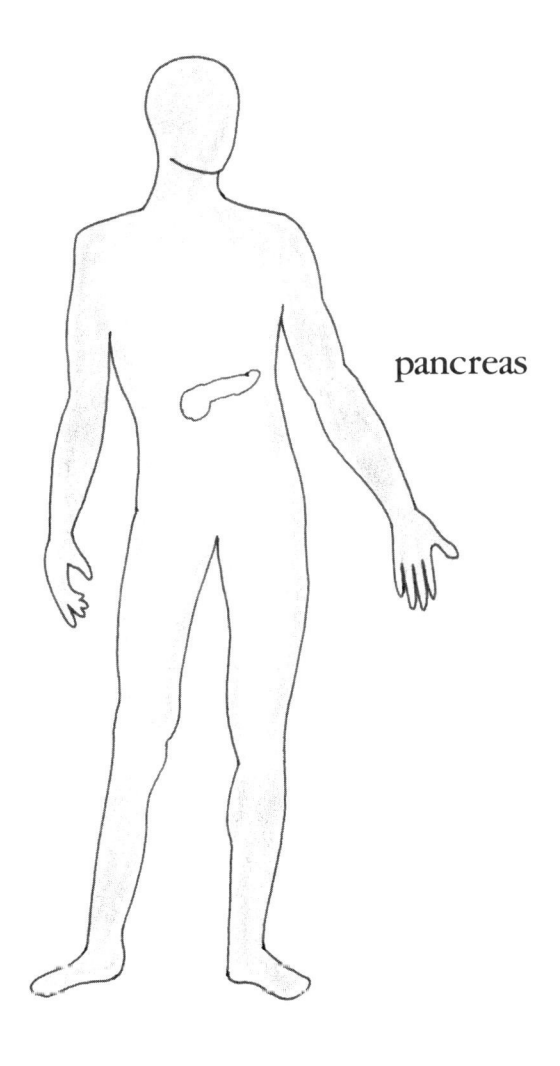

pancreas

Your body needs energy to work right. This energy comes from the food you eat.

When you eat, your body changes food into sugar to use for energy. The sugar goes into the bloodstream and then to all parts of your body.

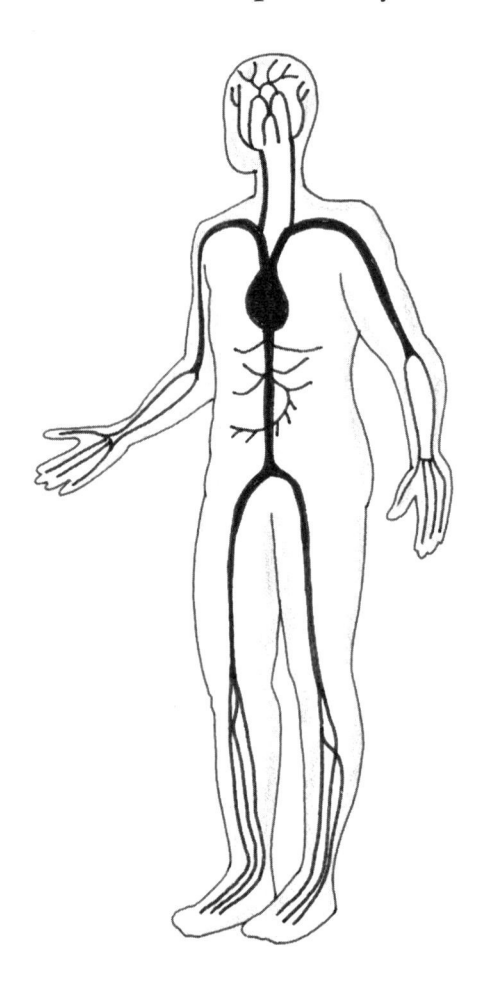

What is Diabetes?

Diabetes is a serious health problem. There is no cure for diabetes, but it can be controlled. You can still have a healthy and active life.

There are many things you need to know about diabetes. This book will help answer some of your questions about diabetes.

What Is Diabetes?

What is Diabetes?
Page 1

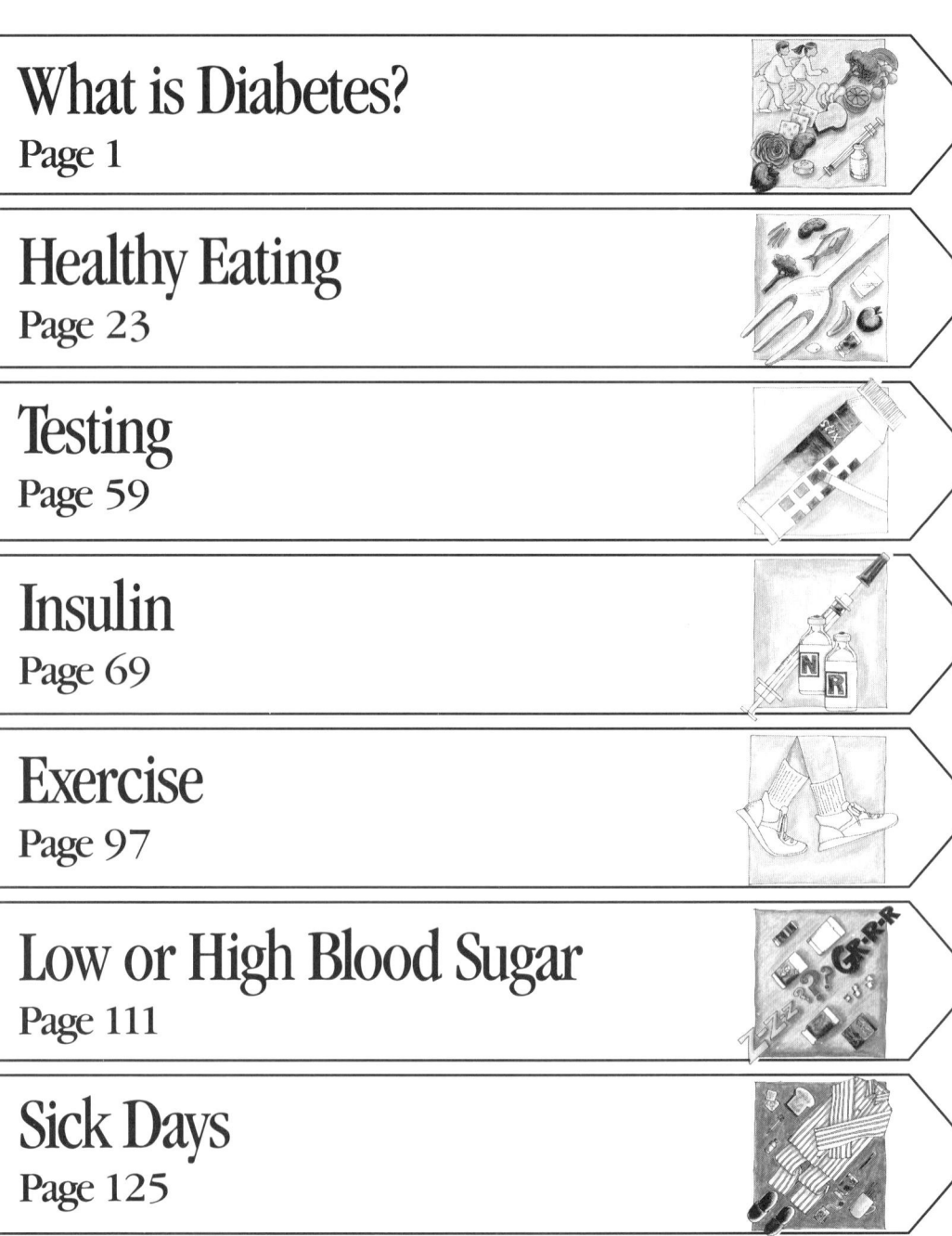

Healthy Eating
Page 23

Testing
Page 59

Insulin
Page 69

Exercise
Page 97

Low or High Blood Sugar
Page 111

Sick Days
Page 125

Foot Care
Page 139

The cells in the body use sugar for energy. Insulin helps sugar get into the cells so it can be used for energy.

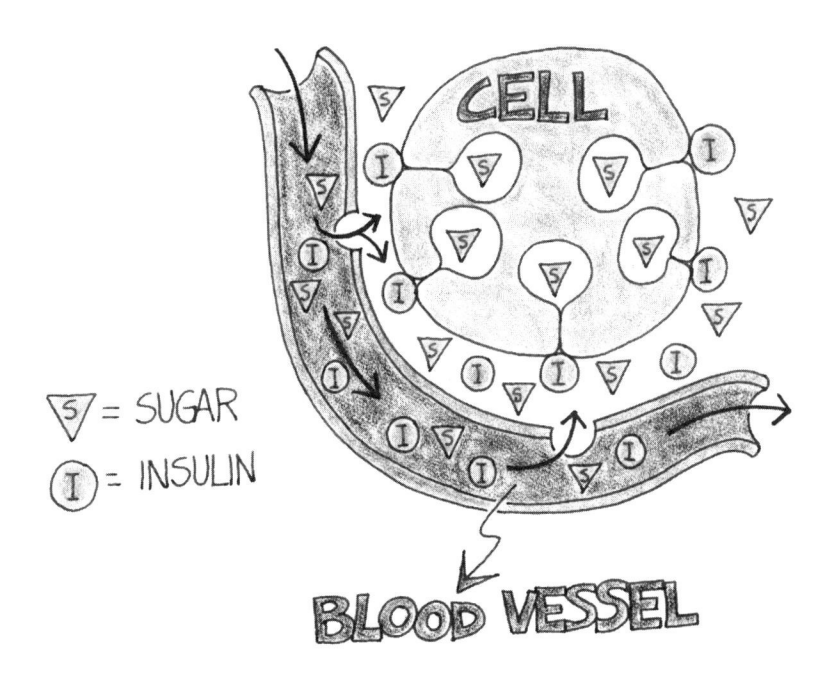

▽ = SUGAR
Ⓘ = INSULIN

Type I and Type II diabetes are the two main kinds of diabetes.

Type I diabetes is also called Insulin-Dependent Diabetes. Type I diabetes usually happens in children and young adults, but can happen at any age.

Type I diabetes is a disease where the body does not make insulin. If you have no insulin, the sugar can't get into the cells for energy. The sugar stays in the bloodstream.

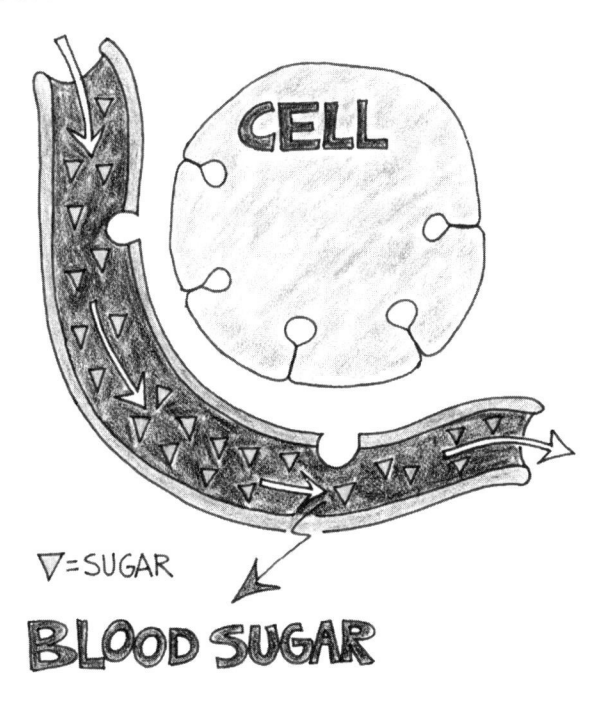

▽ = SUGAR

BLOOD SUGAR

When the sugar in your blood gets too high, your body will tell you:

You could be very thirsty.

You could be very tired.

You could go to the bathroom very often.

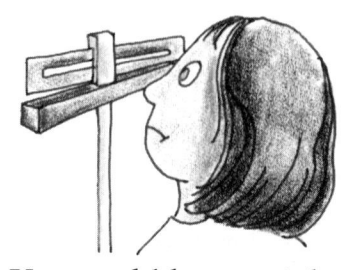

You could lose weight.

You could have fast breathing.

You could be hungry.

You could have

O-o-ow

pain in your stomach.

You could vomit.

Your doctor will do a blood test to find out if your blood sugar is too high. If your blood sugar is high, you have diabetes.

To take care of **Type I** diabetes you will need to:

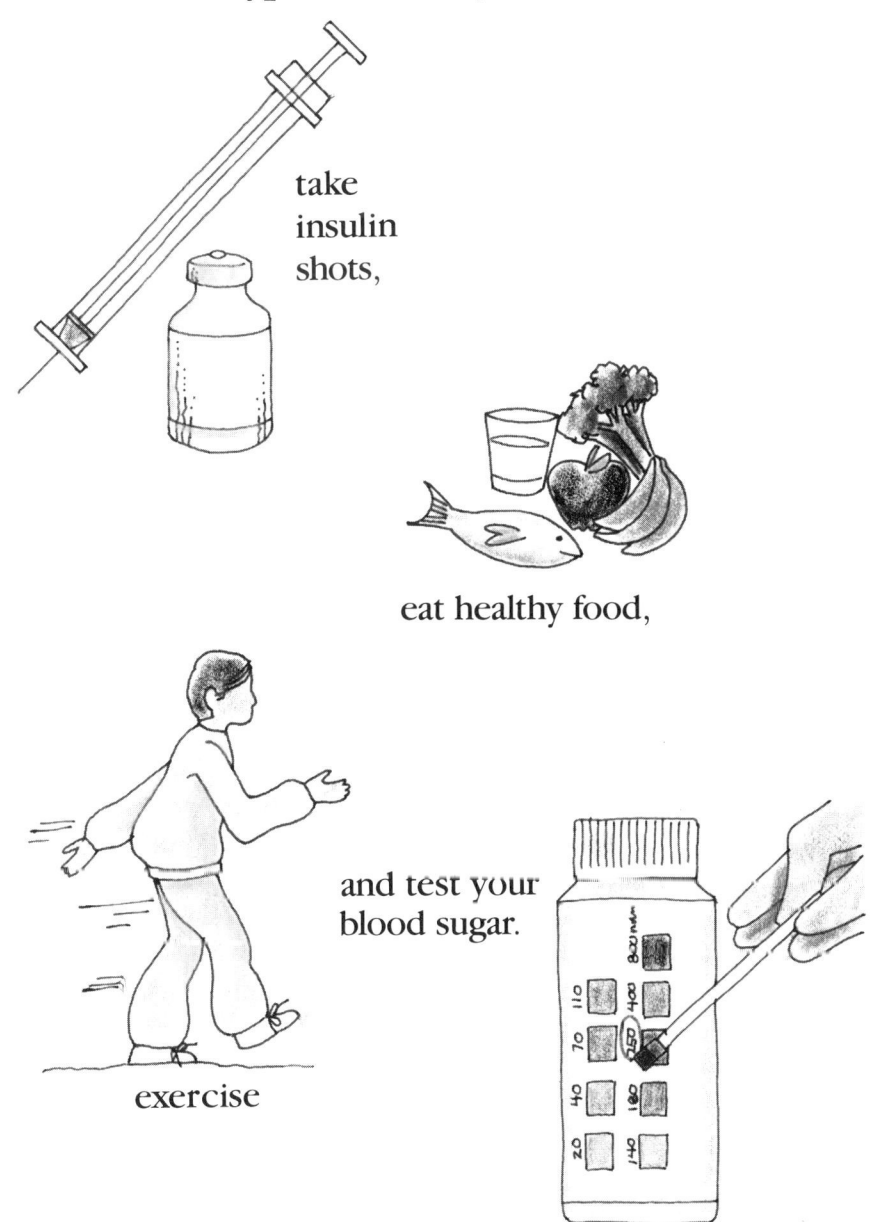

take insulin shots,

eat healthy food,

exercise

and test your blood sugar.

If you do not have the right amount of insulin, food and exercise, you could get a blood sugar that is too low. If your blood sugar gets <u>too low</u>, one of these things could have happened:

>You forgot to eat your meal or snack.
>You did not eat all of your meal or snack.
>You did not eat your meal or snack at the right time.
>You got more exercise than usual.
>You took too much insulin.

If you do not have the right amount of insulin, food and exercise, your blood sugar could also get too high. If your blood sugar gets <u>too high</u>, one of these things could have happened:

>You did not take enough insulin.
>You ate too much food.
>You did not exercise.
>You are sick.

The other kind of diabetes is **Type II** diabetes. It is also called Noninsulin-Dependent Diabetes. Type II diabetes usually happens in adults who weigh too much and are over age 30. Several people in the same family may develop Type II diabetes.

In Type II diabetes, your body still makes some insulin, but it does not work in the right way. If you weigh too much, insulin also does not work in the right way. Most of the sugar can't get into the cells to be used for energy. The sugar stays in the bloodstream.

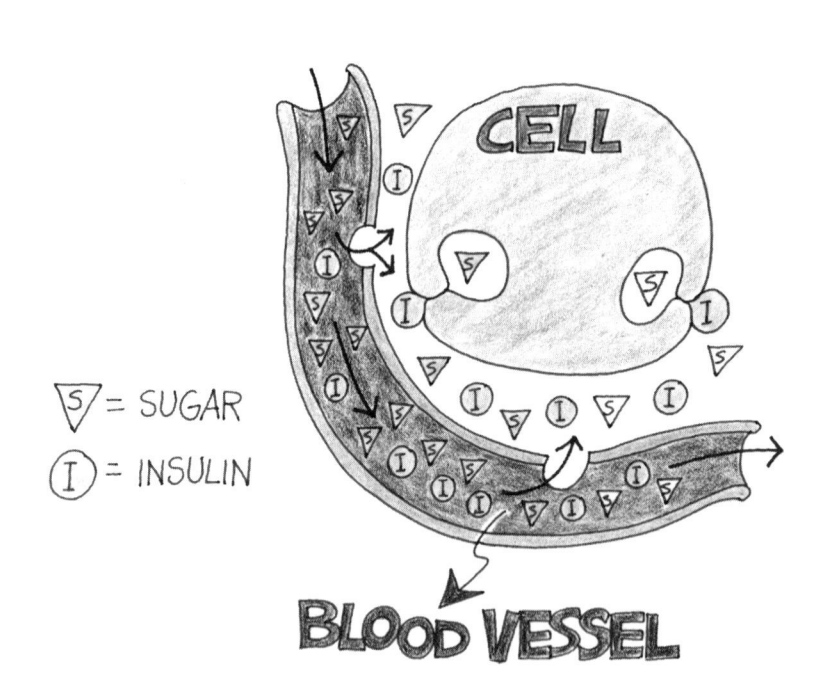

⑤ = SUGAR

Ⓘ = INSULIN

When the sugar in your blood gets too high, usually your body will tell you.

You could be very tired.

You could have blurry vision.

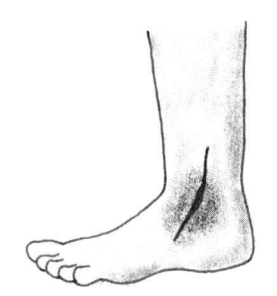

You may have cuts or sores that don't heal.

You may not have these problems and still have diabetes. You may feel the way you always do.

Your doctor will do a blood test to find out if your blood sugar is too high. If your blood sugar is too high, you have diabetes.

To take care of **Type II** diabetes you will need to eat healthy foods and exercise. You may also need to take diabetes pills. Or you may need to take insulin shots. Your doctor will decide if you need diabetes pills or insulin shots. Healthy food, exercise and diabetes pills or insulin shots, in the right amounts, will help keep your blood sugar from being too high or too low. It is also important to test your blood sugar.

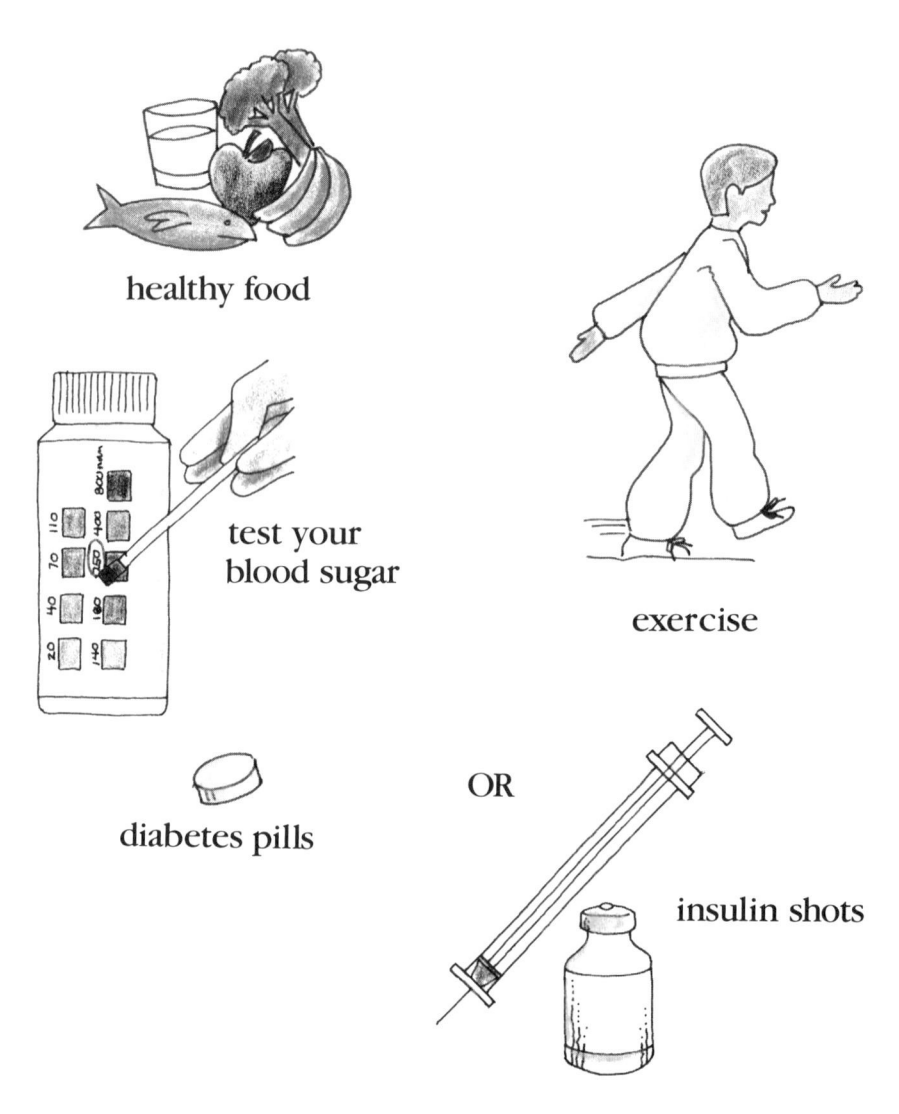

healthy food

test your blood sugar

exercise

diabetes pills OR insulin shots

If you do not have the right amount of food, exercise and diabetes pills or insulin, your blood sugar could get too high. If your blood sugar gets too high, one of these could have happened:

You did not take enough diabetes pills.
Your diabetes pills are not working.
You ate too much food.
You did not exercise.
You are sick.
You may need to take insulin.
If you already take insulin, you
   may need to take more insulin.

Insulin, food and exercise, in the right amounts, will help keep your blood sugar from being too high or too low.

In people who do not have diabetes, blood sugar stays between 70 and 140 mg/dl.

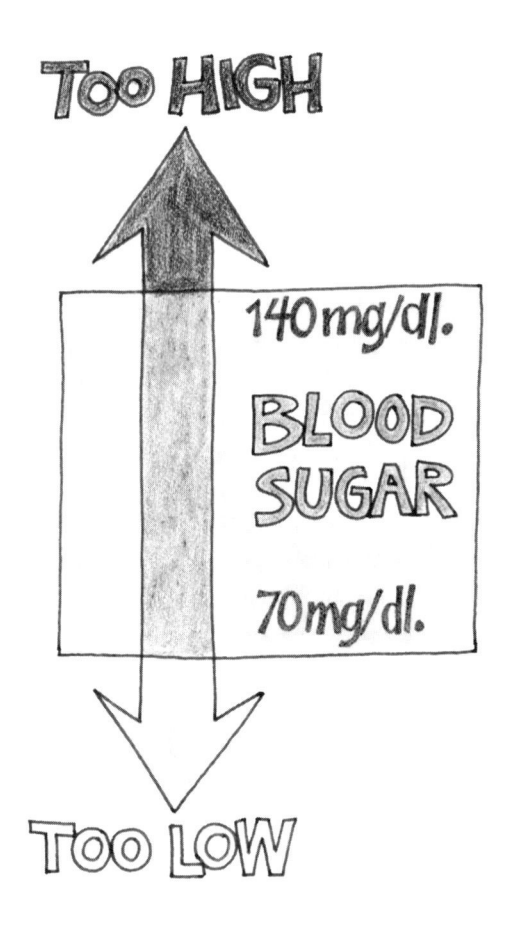

To find out if your blood sugar is right, you will need to test your blood for sugar. This will help you find out if your insulin, food and exercise are working.

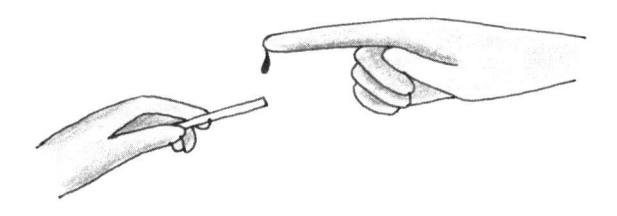

Your doctor or nurse will teach you how to test your blood for sugar. They will also tell you when to do the test.

There are some problems with diabetes that happen slowly over time. These problems may happen if you have high blood sugars over a long time. You may not notice them for months or even years.

After a long time you might get problems with:

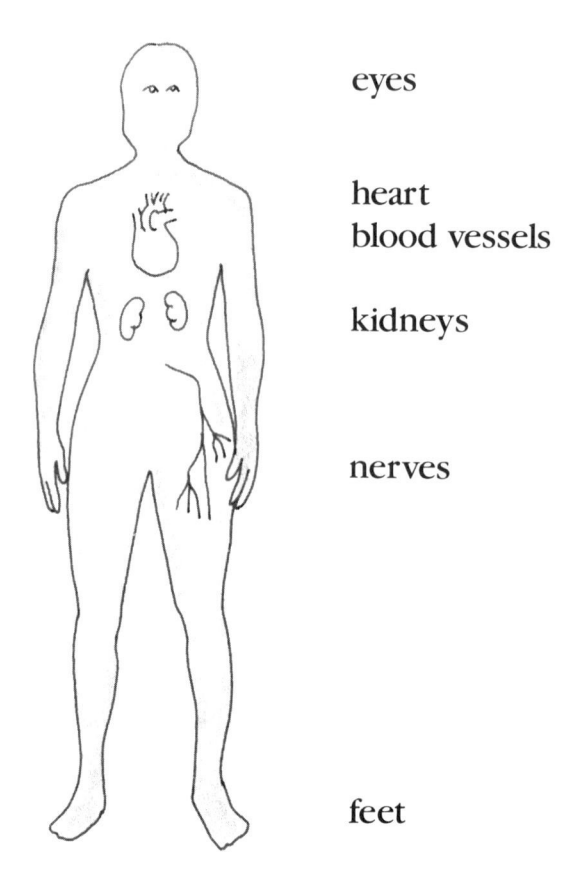

eyes

heart
blood vessels

kidneys

nerves

feet

Diabetes can also cause problems with:

pregnancy

growth in children

Remember, the balance of food, exercise and diabetes pills or insulin shots is very important. This will help you keep your blood sugar from being too high or too low. Keeping your blood sugar just right can keep problems from happening.

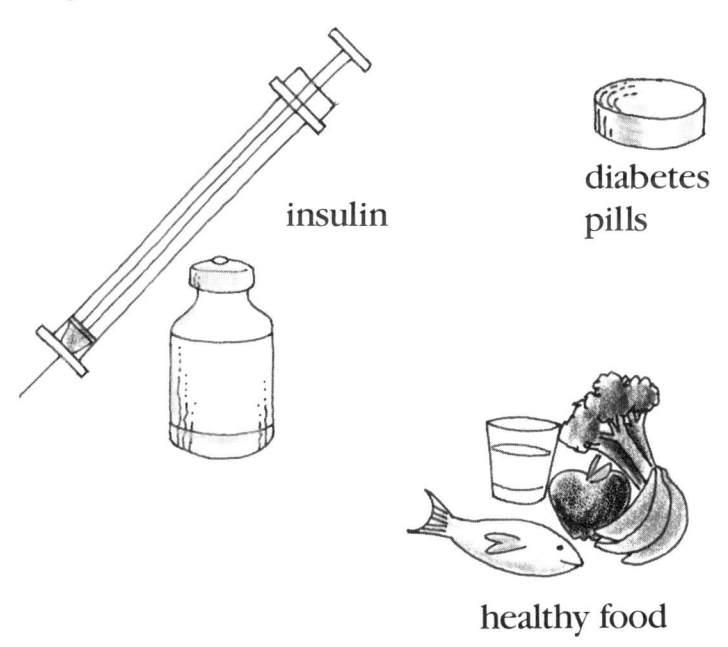

insulin

diabetes pills

healthy food

exercise

Sometimes you will feel angry that you have diabetes. You may get frustrated or sad and ask "Why me?" You may not want to do your blood tests. There may be times when you will not want to eat the right foods.

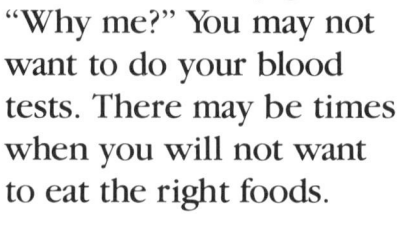

Your doctor or nurse is there to help you through these times. You may also want to see a counselor.

Doctor telephone number _____

Nurse telephone number _____

There are people ready to answer your questions and help you. Remember, you are the one who will know the most about your diabetes. You should have your doctor or nurse see you often and talk to you about your diabetes. They will tell you how often to come see them. You may need to call them between visits if you have questions or problems.

You can live a long, happy and healthy life with diabetes.

Healthy Eating

Healthy Eating

The food you eat and drink can change into blood sugar in your body. Insulin helps your body use the blood sugar for energy. When you do not have enough insulin, your body can not use the sugar for energy. It stays in your blood. Then your blood sugar goes too high.

Here are things to do to help keep your blood sugar normal.

Take your diabetes medicine if your doctor has told you to.

Exercise. Increase your daily activity.

Eat healthy foods in the right amounts.

You need to eat right to help your diabetes. You need to follow a meal plan.

A meal plan will tell you —

What to eat.

How much to eat.

When to eat.

You and your meal planner _____
can plan how you should eat.

Your meal plan will help you in these ways —
    Keep your blood sugar normal.
    Lose weight or stay at a good weight.
    Choose good foods for good health.

What to Eat

Many foods, in the right amounts, are good for you. But there are foods you should not eat or you should eat very little of.

In general: Eat food with fiber

Fresh fruits and vegetables (eat the skins)
Whole grain breads and crackers
Beans, peas, legumes, brown rice, barley, oats, and lentils

Eat starches and grains

Breads, cereals, grains, pastas, potatoes, rice, and starchy vegetables

Eat fruits and vegetables

Fresh, frozen, dried, and canned.

Eat less sugar and sweets

Regular soda pop, sugar, honey, candy, desserts, pastries, regular Jell-O.

Eat less fat

Eat less sausage, bacon, luncheon meats, cold cuts, cheese, fried foods.

Eat less butter, margarine, oil, lard, gravy, salad dressings, mayonnaise.

Cut the fat off of meat before cooking.

Eat small servings of meat.

Drink skim milk or 1% milk.

Eat low fat cheese.

How Much to Eat

To help your diabetes, you need to lose weight or stay at a good weight.

Today you weigh _____.

A good weight for you is _____.

You need to eat the right amounts of food to weigh this much.

Your meal planner can tell you exactly how much food to eat at each meal or snack.

To know how much food you should eat you can use these things.

Measuring cups

Measuring spoons

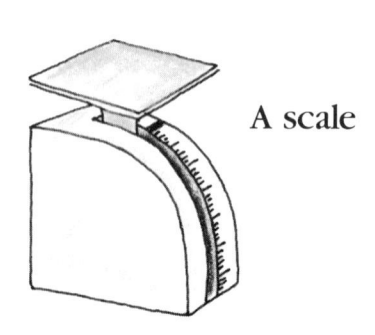

A scale

If you cannot measure the food you eat, remember these things.

Keep meat portions small. About the size of a deck of cards.

Eat only one helping. No seconds.

Keep serving sizes small.

Eat only one to two starchy foods at each meal.

Do not add extra fats to foods – margarine, butter, sour cream, gravy.

When to Eat

Eating at the right time each day will help your diabetes. You need to spread out your meals and snacks to help keep your blood sugar normal. You and your meal planner can plan your meal and snack times to fit how you live.

Remember:

Eat at about the same time every day.

Do not skip meals or snacks.

Take your diabetes medicine at about the same time every day.

Follow the meal plan you and your meal planner have set up for you.

Breakfast   Snack   Lunch/Dinner

If you take insulin:

Take your insulin at about the same time every day.

Eat your meals and snacks at about the same time every day.

Do not skip meals or any part of them.

Do not skip snacks or any part of them.

If your meal is more than one hour late, eat a small snack.

> one piece of fruit, or
> a small glass of juice, or
> four to six crackers, or
> one slice of bread,

Then eat your meal as soon as you can.

Follow the meal plan you and your meal planner have set up for you.

Snack   Supper   Snack

Starches and grains

Good for you

Breads
    Whole wheat
    Cracked wheat
    Rye
    Pumpernickel
    White
    Sourdough
    Cornbread
    Bagels

Grains
    Brown rice
    Rice
    Wild rice
    Barley
    Buckwheat (kasha)
    Bulgur
    Oatmeal
    Cornmeal
    Hominy
    Corn

Not as Good for you

Breads with frosting or icing

Fry bread

Breads fried in fat

Breads with cheese in them

Sweet rolls

Doughnuts

Pastries

Fritters

Stuffing or dressing

Hush puppies

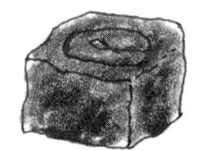

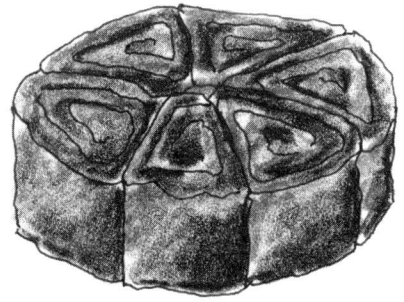

Starches and grains

Good for you

Cereals
   Hot and cold
     cereals
   Grits

Potatoes
   Baked
   Boiled
   Mashed

Sweet potatoes
Yams
Pasta
Tortillas
Crackers
Graham crackers
Pretzels
Popcorn – no butter
   or margarine

Not as Good for you

Sugar cereals (sugar coated)

Scalloped potatoes
Creamed potatoes
Au gratin potatoes
Fried potatoes
Hash browns

Potato chips/Fritos

Meats and proteins

Good for you

Lean cuts of:
    Beef
    Lamb
    Pork
    Veal

Chicken and turkey

Wild game

Fish and shellfish

Not as Good for you

Prime cuts of:
  Beef
  Lamb
  Pork
  Veal

Sausages
Lunch meats
Bologna
Salami
Spam

Tongue, brain, liver, kidney

Ham hocks
Pigs feet
Chittlins
Salt pork

Any meat that is fried or deep fried

Peanut butter
  (more than one spoonful)

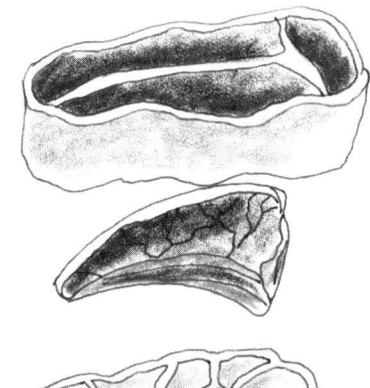

Meats and proteins

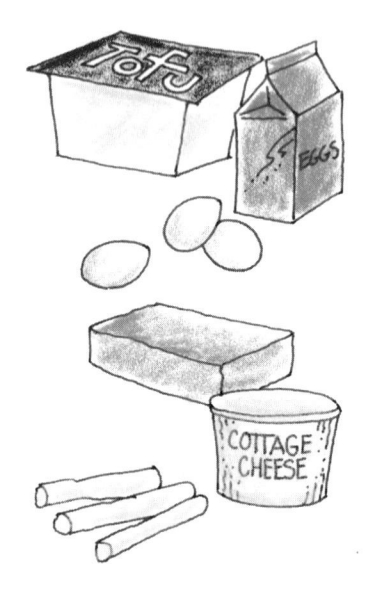

Good for you

Tofu

Eggs or egg substitute

Low fat cheese
  Skim milk cheese
  Mozzarella
  String cheese
  Farmers cheese
  1% or 2% cottage cheese

Hints:

Cut the fat off of meat before cooking.

Cut the skin off of chicken before cooking.

Bake, broil, roast or grill meat to let the fat drip off.

Eat four eggs or less per week.

Not as Good for you

Fried eggs
Scrambled eggs with added fat

High fat cheese
    Cheddar
    Swiss
    American
    Monterey Jack
    Colby
    Cream cheese
    Head cheese
    Goat cheese
    Cheese spreads

Vegetables

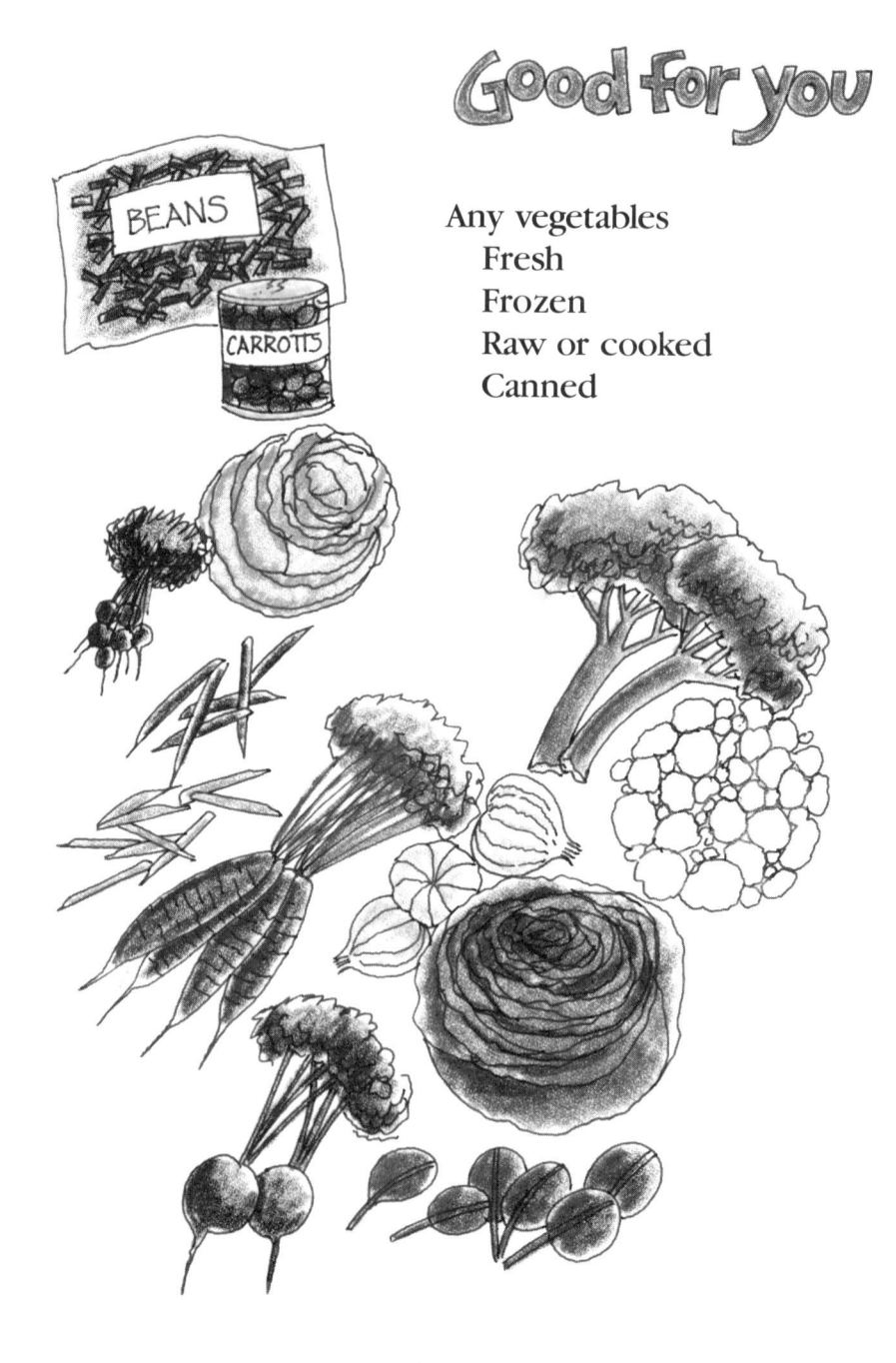

Good for you

Any vegetables
- Fresh
- Frozen
- Raw or cooked
- Canned

Not as Good for you

- Vegetables with cream sauce
- Vegetables with cheese sauce
- Vegetables with butter or margarine
- Fried vegetables
- Sweet pickles

Fruits

Good for you

Any fruits
 Fresh
 Dried
 Frozen
 Canned (in water or fruit juice)

Juices with no sugar added

Not as Good for you

Frozen with sugar added

Canned in light or heavy syrup

Fruit drinks
- Koolaid made with sugar
- Hi-C
- Tang

Fruit punch

Lemonade

Limeade

Milk Foods

Good for you

Skim milk
1% milk
Buttermilk
Powdered milk
Nonfat dry milk
Evaporated skim milk
Ice milk (one scoop)

Plain, low-fat yogurt
Frozen yogurt (one scoop)

Artificially sweetened fruited yogurt

Not as Good for you

Whole milk
2% milk
Goats milk
Condensed milk
Chocolate milk

Ice cream

Shakes and malts

Fruited or flavored yogurt

Fats

Good for you

Margarine

Oils
- Corn
- Safflower
- Sunflower
- Soybean
- Peanut
- Olive

Low calorie, reduced calorie or diet:
- Salad dressings
- Mayonnaise
- Margarine

Lower fat salad dressings
- Oil and vinegar
- French

Remember – eat less fat of any kind.

Not as Good for you

Butter

Lard
Shortening
Bacon drippings
Fat back

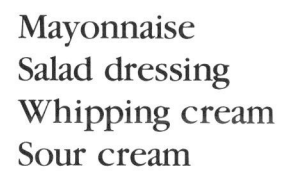

Mayonnaise
Salad dressing
Whipping cream
Sour cream

Cream-like salad dressing
- 1000 Island
- Blue cheese

Dips made from sour cream or mayonnaise

Gravy
Cream sauces
Cheese sauces

Sweets and desserts

Good for you

Fruit
Sugar free soda pop

Sugar free Jell-O
Sugar free pudding

NutraSweet
Equal
Sweet 'N Low
Sweet One
Swiss Sweet

Low sugar jam
   or jelly

Sugar free syrup

Graham crackers
   (three squares)
Vanilla wafers (six)
Angel food cake
   (one small piece)
Cookie (one)
Ice milk
   (one scoop)
Frozen yogurt
   (one scoop)

Not as Good for you

Regular soda pop

Cake, pie, pastries

Doughnuts, ice cream, Jell-O

Pudding

Sugar
   White, brown, powdered

Jam, jelly, preserves

Honey

Syrup
Corn syrup
Molasses

Candy

You can eat these foods in addition to your meal plan. They contain very few calories and have little effect on your blood sugar.

Bouillon or broth without fat
Sugar free soda pop
Carbonated water, mineral water, sparkling water
Club soda
Coffee
Tea
Sugar free fruit drink mixes
Sugar free tonic water

Sugar free Jell-O
Sugar free gum
Saccharin
NutraSweet™
Equal™
Sweet 'N Low™

Cabbage
Celery
Chinese cabbage
Cucumber
Green onion
Hot peppers
Mushrooms
Radishes
Zucchini

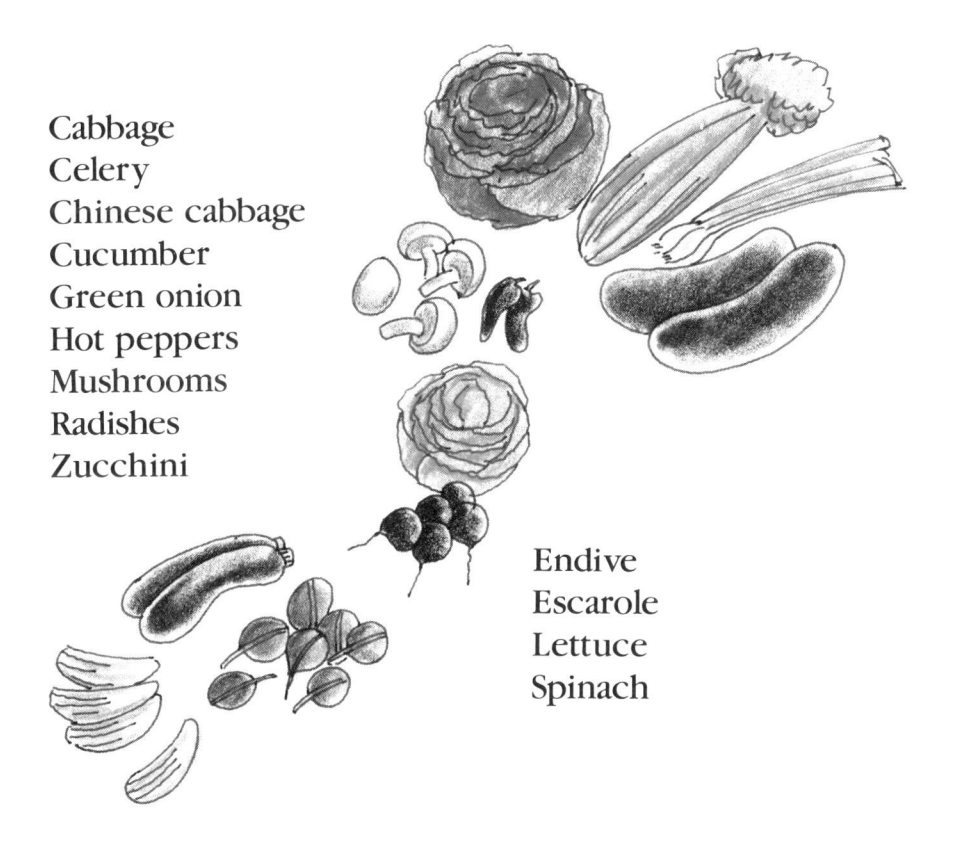

Endive
Escarole
Lettuce
Spinach

Horseradish
Mustard
Pickles (dill, sour)
Vinegar

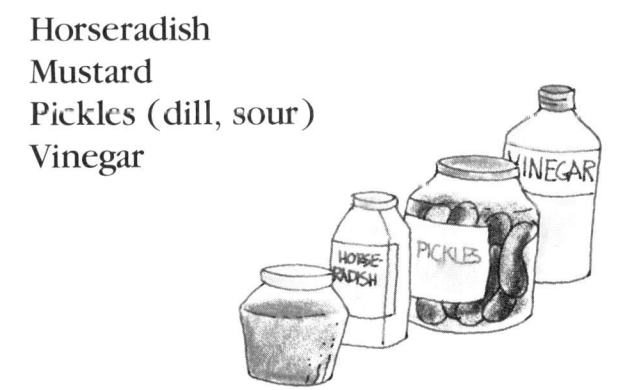

Foods to use in small amounts

Cocoa powder —
 one spoonful

Low sugar jam or jelly —
 two small spoonfuls

Sugar free syrup —
 one to two spoonfuls

Whipped topping —
 two spoonfuls

Catsup —
 one spoonful

Hot sauce —
 one spoonful

Taco sauce —
 one spoonful

Eat the following for
your breakfast:

_____
_____
_____
_____
_____
_____
_____
_____

Breakfast

Eat the following for
your morning snack:

_____
_____
_____

Snack

Eat the following for
your lunch:

_____
_____
_____
_____
_____
_____
_____
_____
_____

Eat the following for
your afternoon snack:

_____
_____
_____
_____

Eat the following for your supper:

_____
_____
_____
_____
_____
_____
_____
_____
_____

Supper

Eat the following for your evening snack:

_____
_____
_____
_____
_____

Snack

Call this number if you have any problems or questions:

_____

Name:

_____

Testing

Testing

You can test your blood sugar to find out if your blood sugar is where it should be. If your blood sugar is too high or too low, you may need a change in your food, exercise or diabetes medicine. Your doctor or nurse will help you with this. They will tell you when to test your blood sugar.

There are two ways to test your blood sugar:
    1. Visual testing
    2. Meter testing

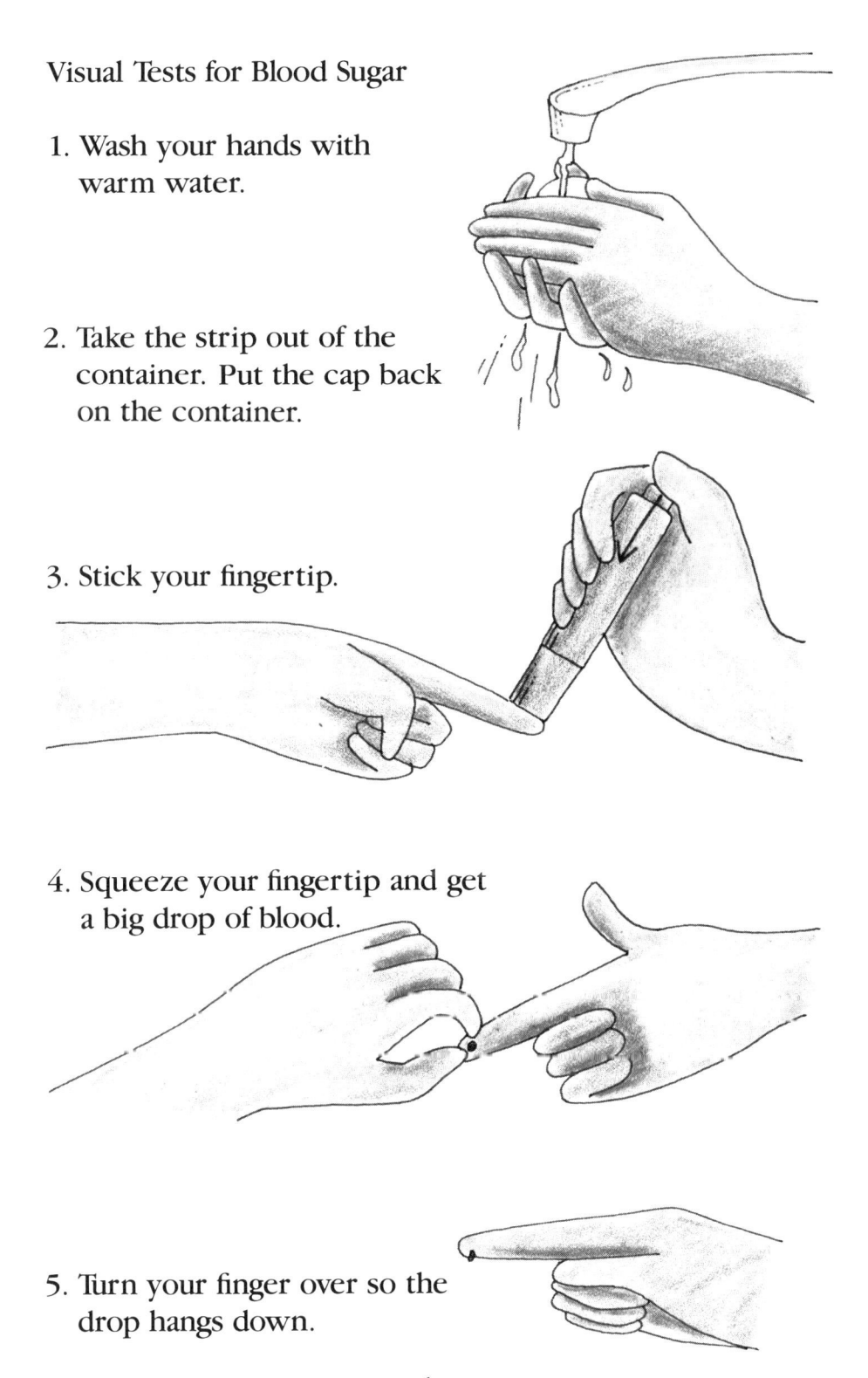

Visual Tests for Blood Sugar

1. Wash your hands with warm water.

2. Take the strip out of the container. Put the cap back on the container.

3. Stick your fingertip.

4. Squeeze your fingertip and get a big drop of blood.

5. Turn your finger over so the drop hangs down.

6. Hold the finger over the pad of the strip.

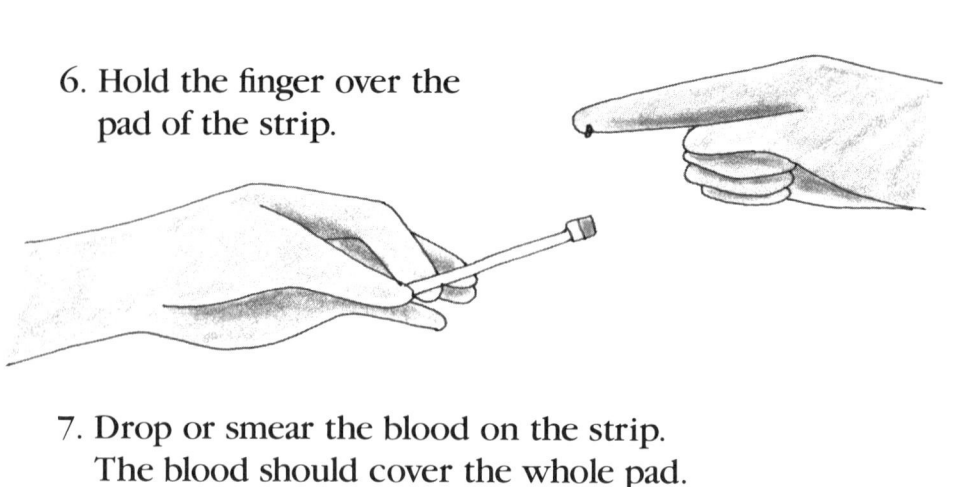

7. Drop or smear the blood on the strip. The blood should cover the whole pad.

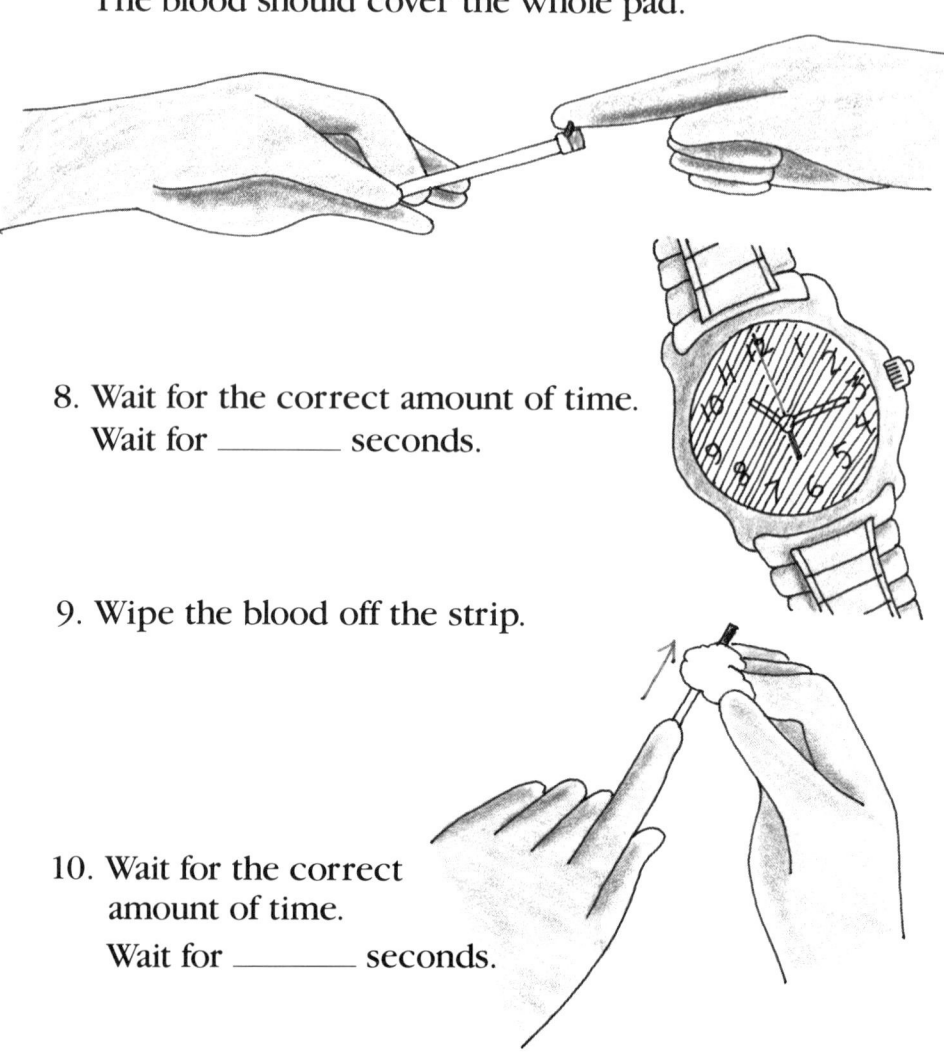

8. Wait for the correct amount of time.
   Wait for _____ seconds.

9. Wipe the blood off the strip.

10. Wait for the correct amount of time.
    Wait for _____ seconds.

11. Put the strip next to the color chart on the bottle. Read the number that matches the color of the pad of the test strip.

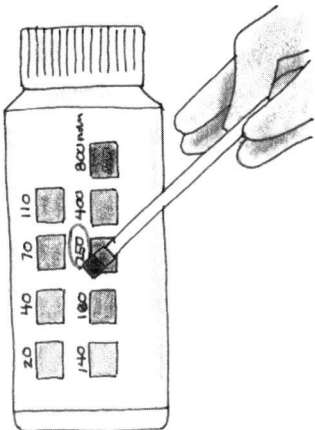

12. Write your blood sugar number in your record book.

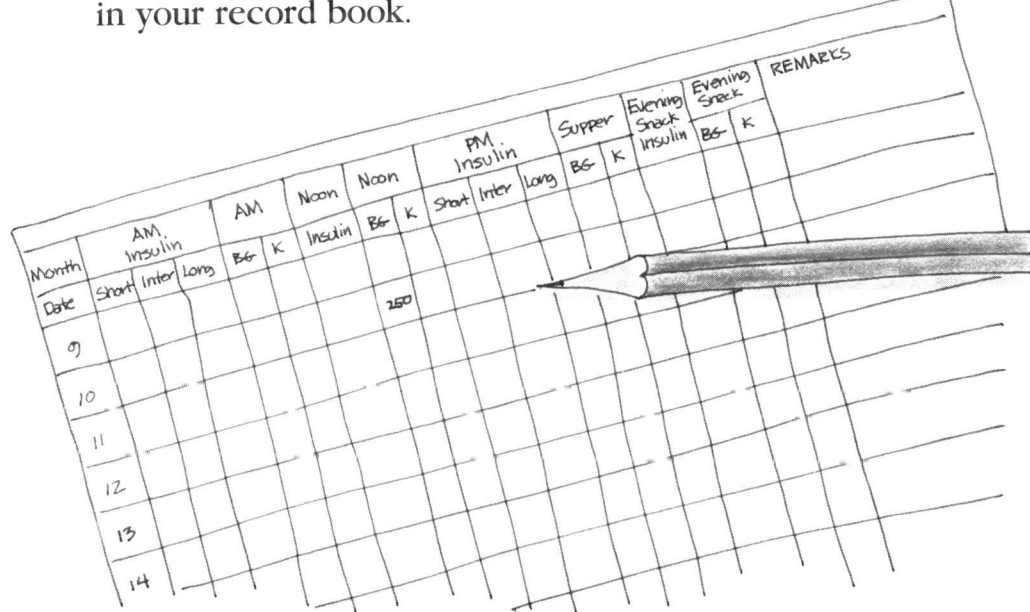

63

Meter Testing for Blood Sugar

1. Follow steps 1-5 for visual testing to get a big drop of blood.

2. Your nurse will teach you how to use a meter.

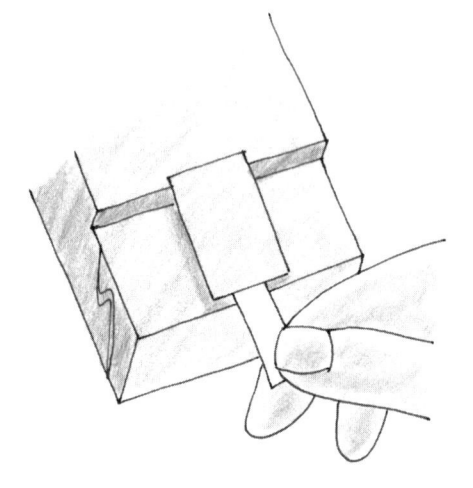

3. The meter shows your blood sugar in its window.

Urine Test for Ketones

Ketones are made in the blood when the body can't get enough energy from sugar and starts to use fat for energy. When fat is used, ketones are made. These ketones build up in the blood and spill into the urine. This usually means you need more insulin. High blood sugars and ketones cause a problem called ketoacidosis.

Test your urine for ketones when:

- your blood sugar is above 240 mg/dl
- you feel sick or have a cold, flu, or infection.

If ketones are positive, check with your doctor to find out what changes you need to make.

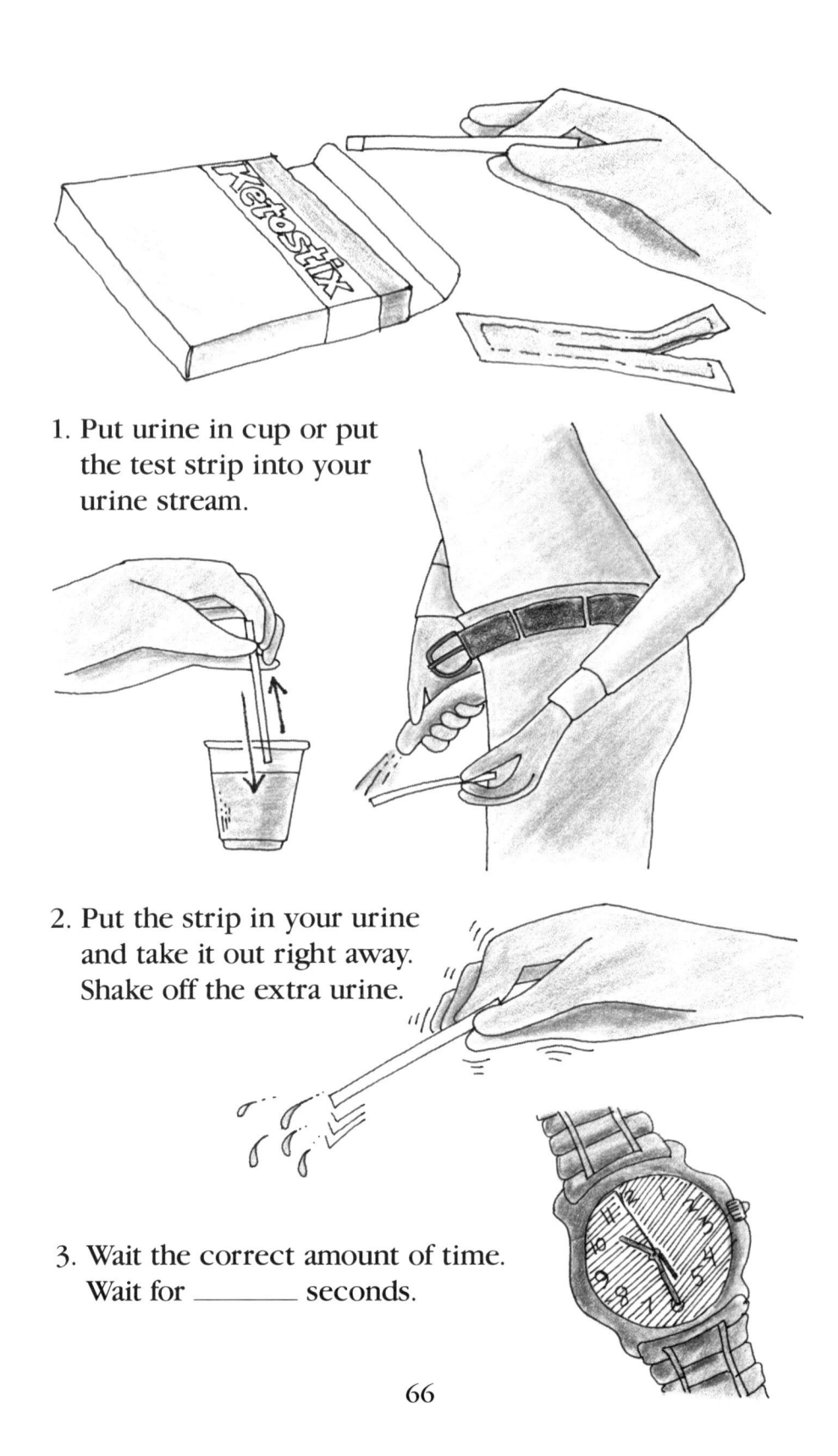

1. Put urine in cup or put the test strip into your urine stream.

2. Put the strip in your urine and take it out right away. Shake off the extra urine.

3. Wait the correct amount of time. Wait for _____ seconds.

4. Put the strip next to the color chart. Read the word that matches the color of the pad of the test strip. This is the amount of ketones in your urine.

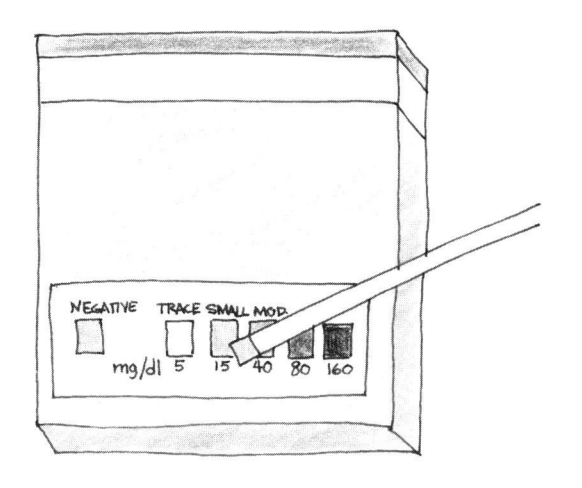

5. Write the word in your record book. If your blood sugar is over 240 mg/dl and there are ketones in your urine, you need to call your doctor.

Record Keeping

It is important to keep good records of your sugar and ketone tests. This will help you and your doctor make changes in insulin, diabetes pills, food or exercise.

Write down the following:
- Date and time of test
- Test results
- Anything different that may have caused your blood sugar to change (illness, stress, too much food, missed meal, a lot of exercise, etc.)

Insulin

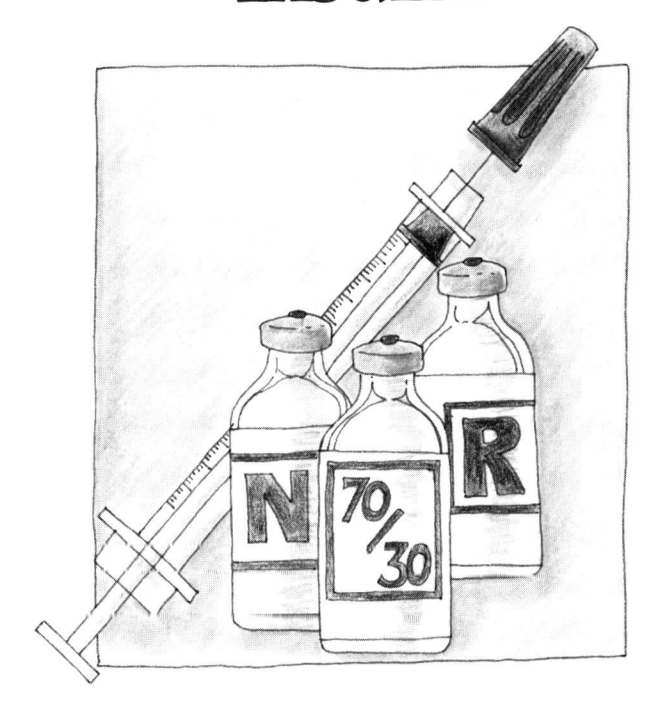

Insulin

When you have diabetes, your body doesn't use sugar the right way. You need insulin to keep your blood sugar normal. Insulin keeps the blood sugar down.

Kinds of Insulin

There are different kinds of insulin:
- Rapid-acting
- Intermediate-acting
- Long-acting, or a
- Combination of intermediate-acting and rapid-acting, 70/30.

Rapid-acting insulin starts to work one-half hour after you give your shot. It works the hardest 2 to 4 hours after you give your shot.

Regular is a rapid-acting insulin.

Intermediate-acting insulin starts acting a little later, but lasts longer. It works the hardest 8 to 10 hours after you give your shot.

NPH and Lente are intermediate-acting insulins.

Intermediate-acting and rapid-acting insulins have also been combined. This is called 70/30.

You will probably take more than one shot of insulin each day. More than one type of insulin may also be used.

You can learn how to give yourself an insulin shot. To give yourself an insulin shot you need your insulin. We measure insulin in units. You need a syringe, too. There are three kinds of syringes.

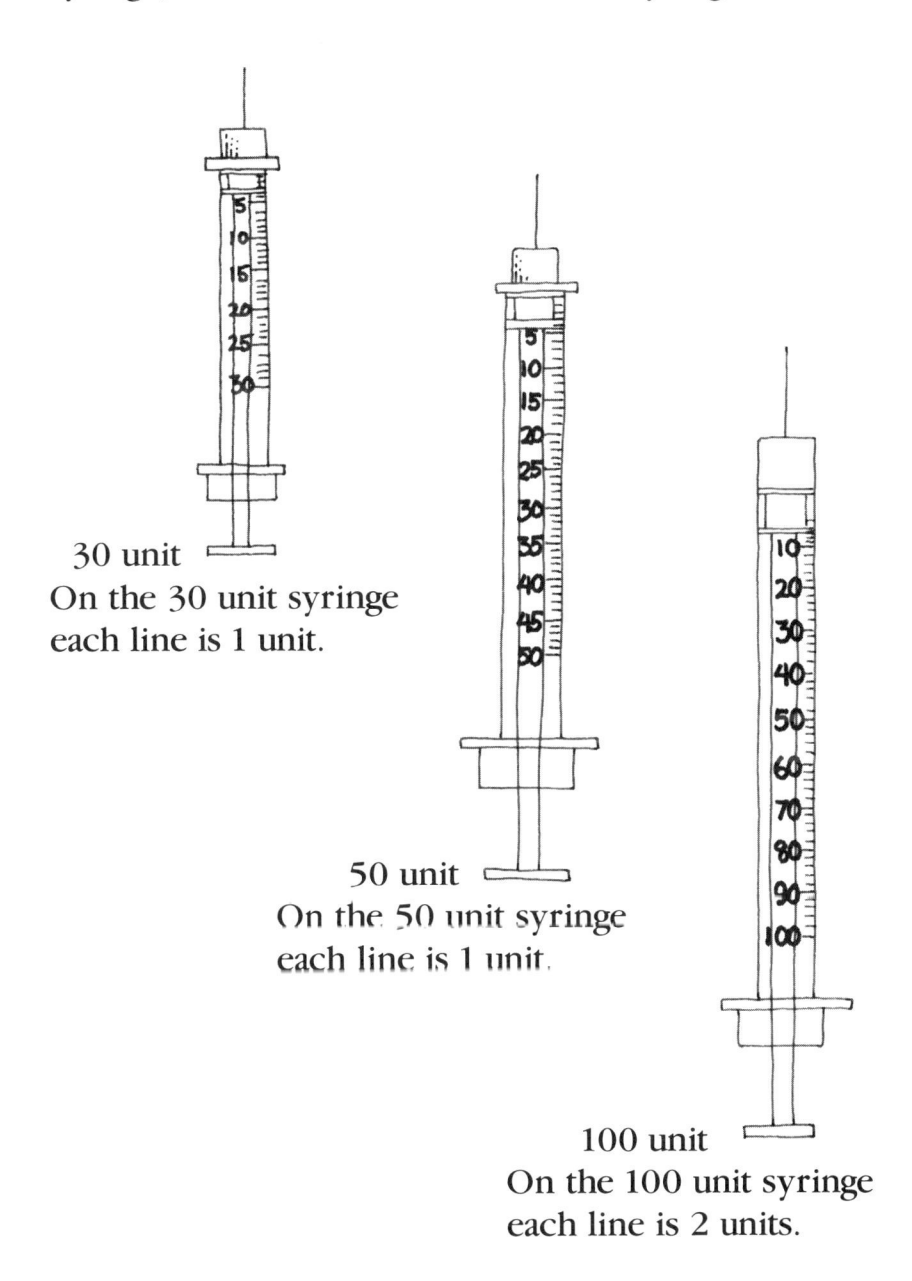

30 unit
On the 30 unit syringe each line is 1 unit.

50 unit
On the 50 unit syringe each line is 1 unit.

100 unit
On the 100 unit syringe each line is 2 units.

The kind of insulin you take is:
_____
_____

At breakfast you will take:

_____ units of _____ and
_____ units of _____.

At lunch you will take:

_____ units of _____ and
_____ units of _____.

At supper you will take:

_____ units of _____ and
_____ units of _____.

At bedtime you will take:

_____ units of _____ and
_____ units of _____.

An insulin shot is given in the fatty part under the skin. Here are the places to give your shot:

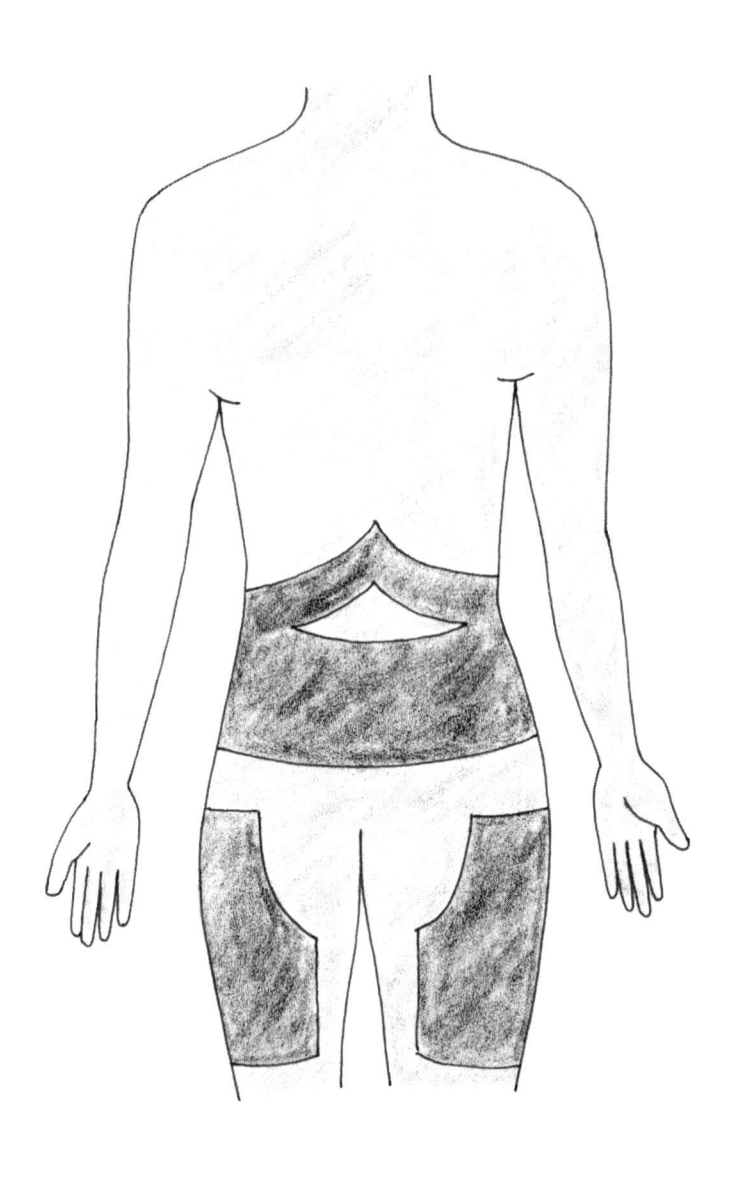

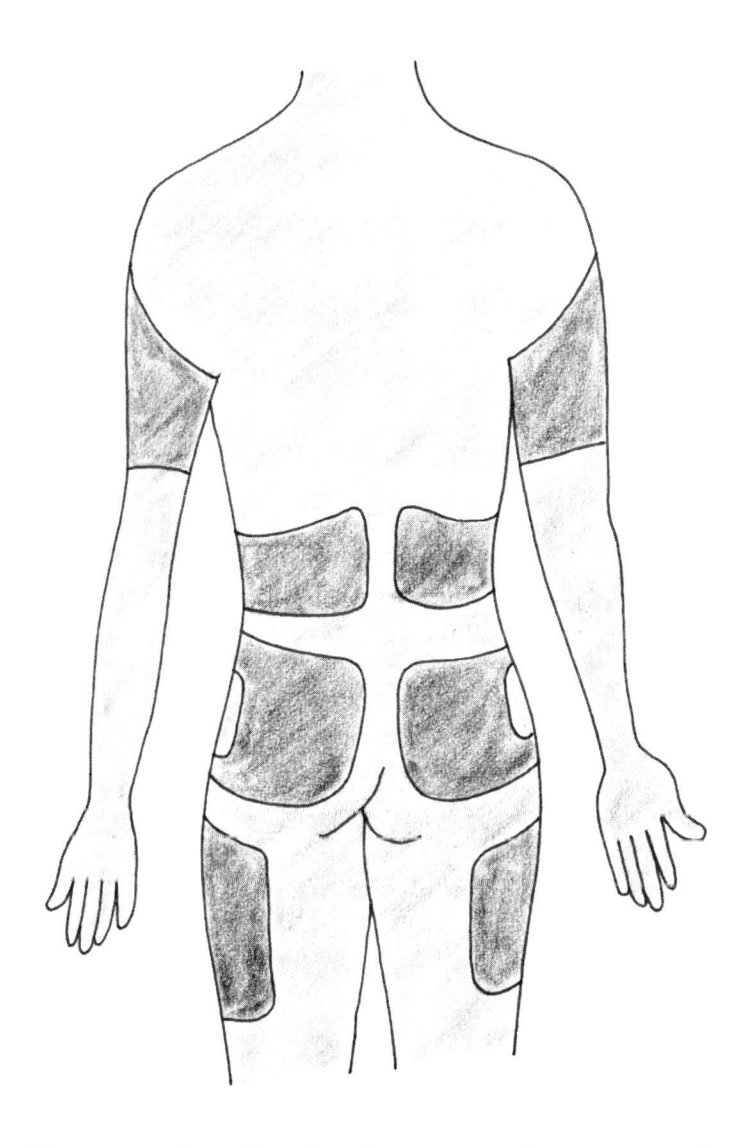

Give your insulin shot in a new place every day.

To give a shot of one kind of insulin, do the following:

1. Get your things together.

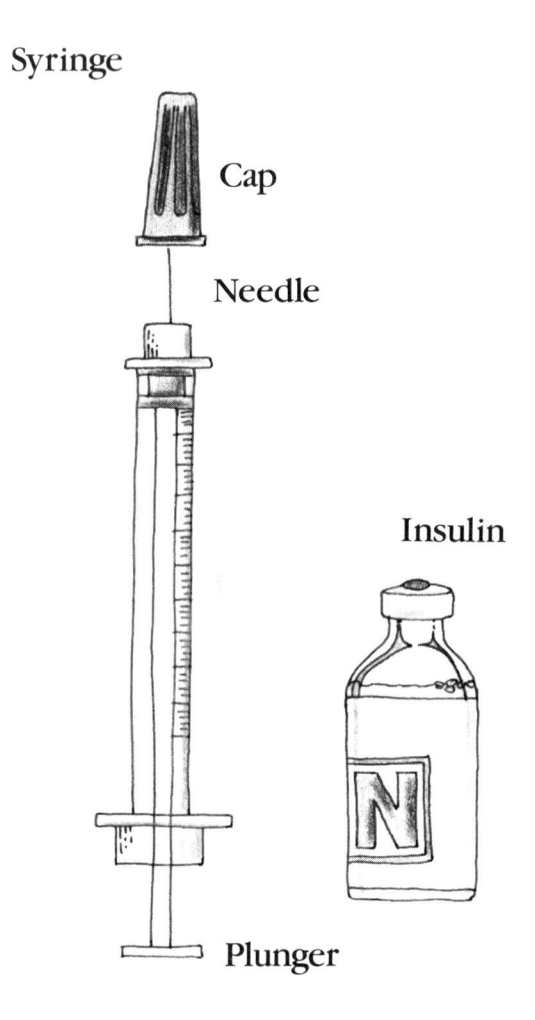

Syringe

Cap

Needle

Insulin

Plunger

2. Wash your hands.

3. Roll the bottle of insulin between your hands.

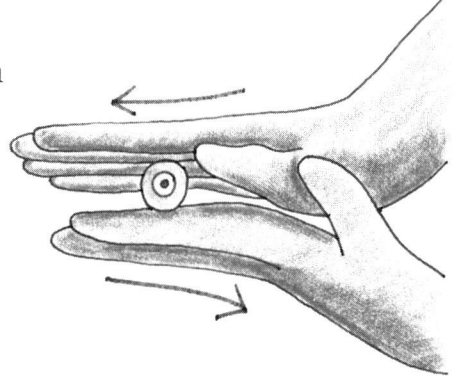

4. Take the cap off of the needle.

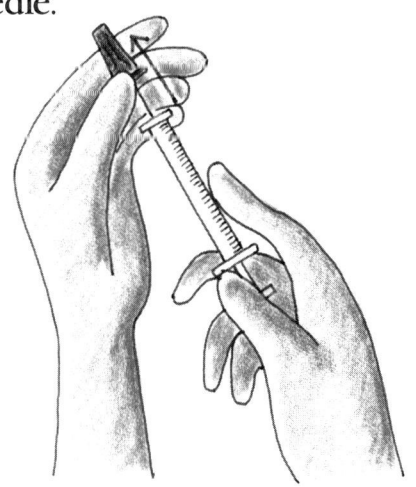

5. Pull the plunger out to ____ units to let air in the syringe. (You need air in the syringe so you can put air into the insulin bottle. You need to put air into the insulin bottle so you can take insulin out of the bottle.)

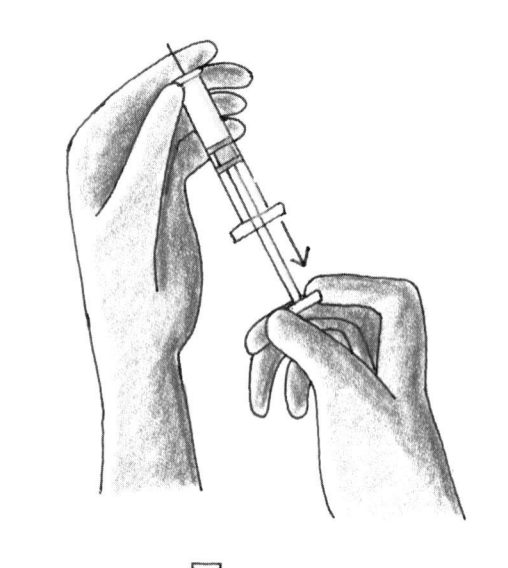

6. Put the needle into the bottle of insulin.

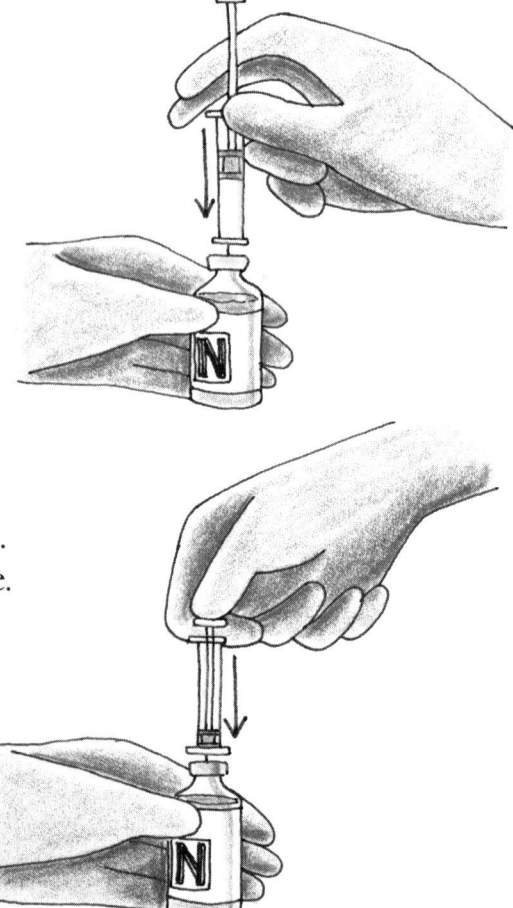

7. Push the plunger down. Shoot air into the bottle.

8. Turn the bottle of insulin upside down with the needle in it. (Be sure the tip of the needle is in the insulin.)

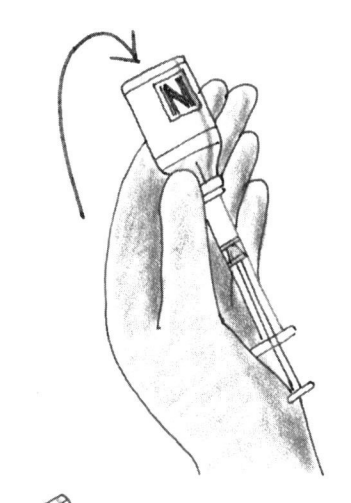

9. Pull the plunger out past the amount you take. Push the insulin back into the bottle. Do this two times.

    Then pull the plunger out to _____ units of insulin.

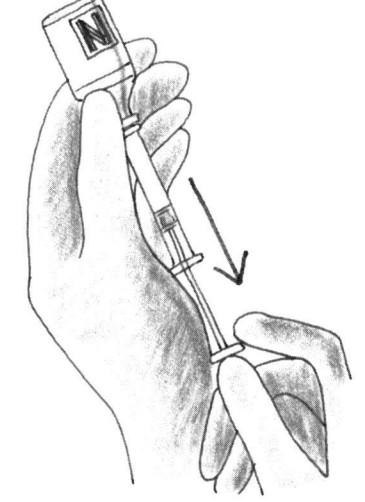

10. Check for air bubbles (Air bubbles do not hurt you, but they mean you get less insulin.) If you have air bubbles, push the insulin back into the bottle and start from number 9.

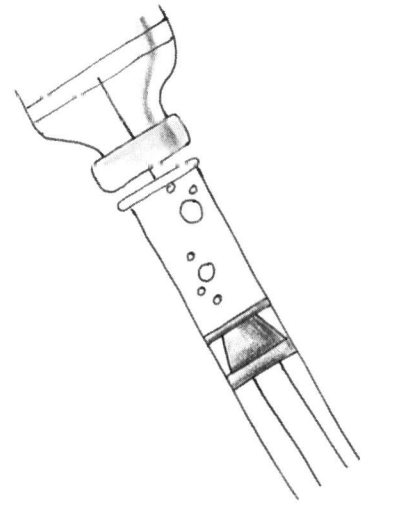

11. When you have _____ units of insulin in the syringe with no air bubbles, you can take the needle out of the bottle.

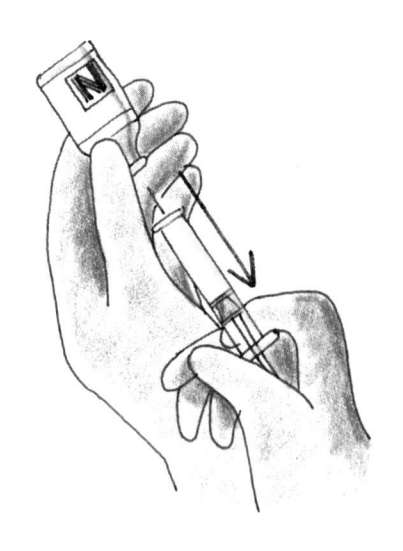

12. Now you are ready to give your shot.

Give your insulin shot in a new place every day.
Give your shot this way:

Pinch up your skin.

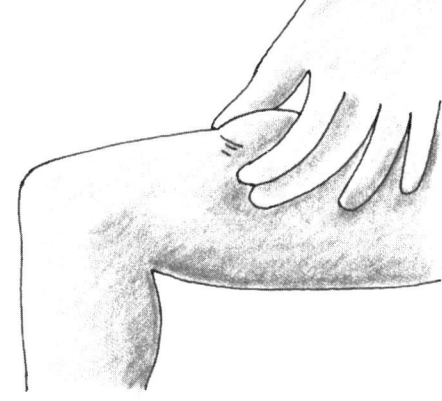

Push the needle through your skin.

Let go of the pinch.

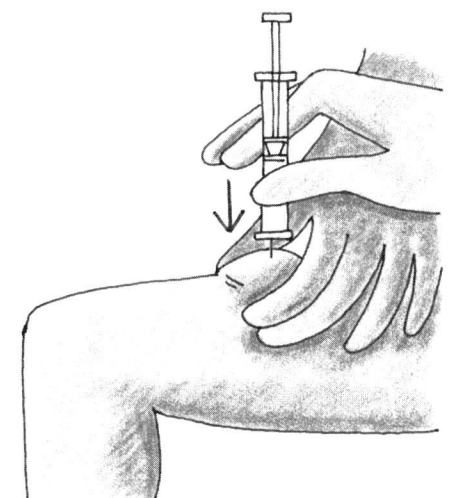

Push the plunger down.

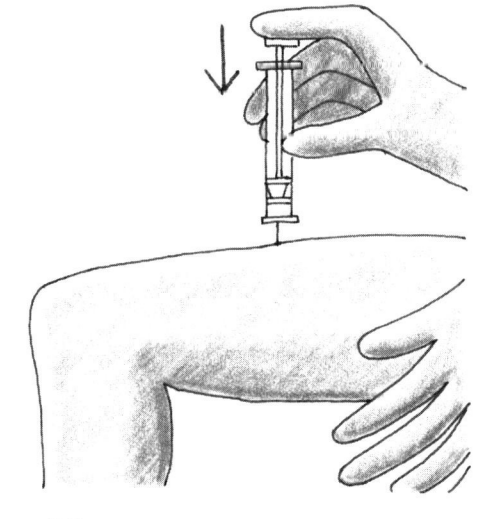

Take the needle out of your skin.

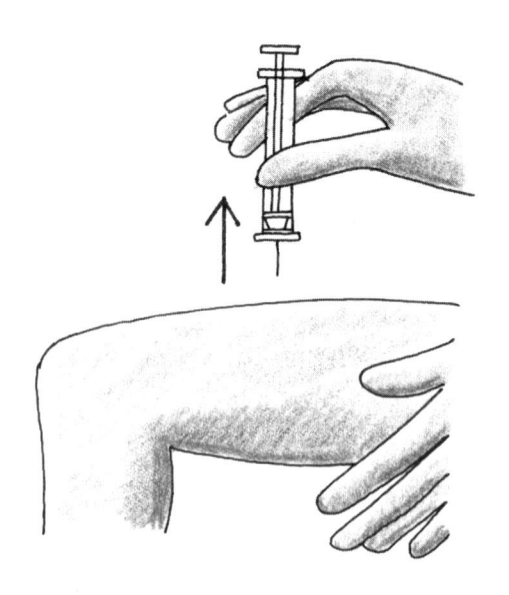

Put your finger over the place you gave your shot.

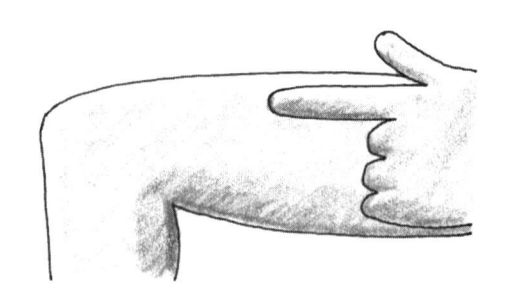

Take your insulin at

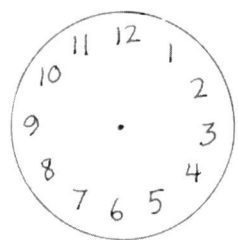

To give a shot of two kinds of insulin, do the following:

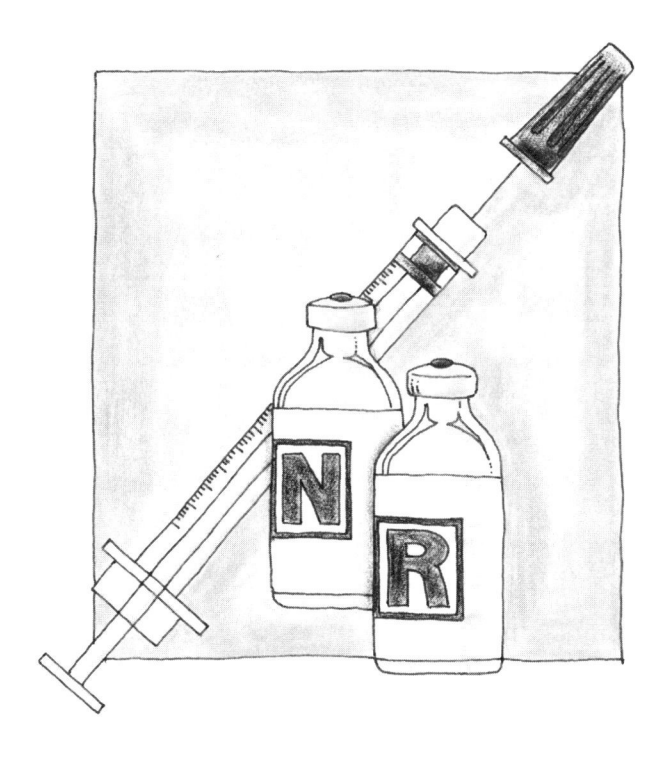

1. Get your things together.

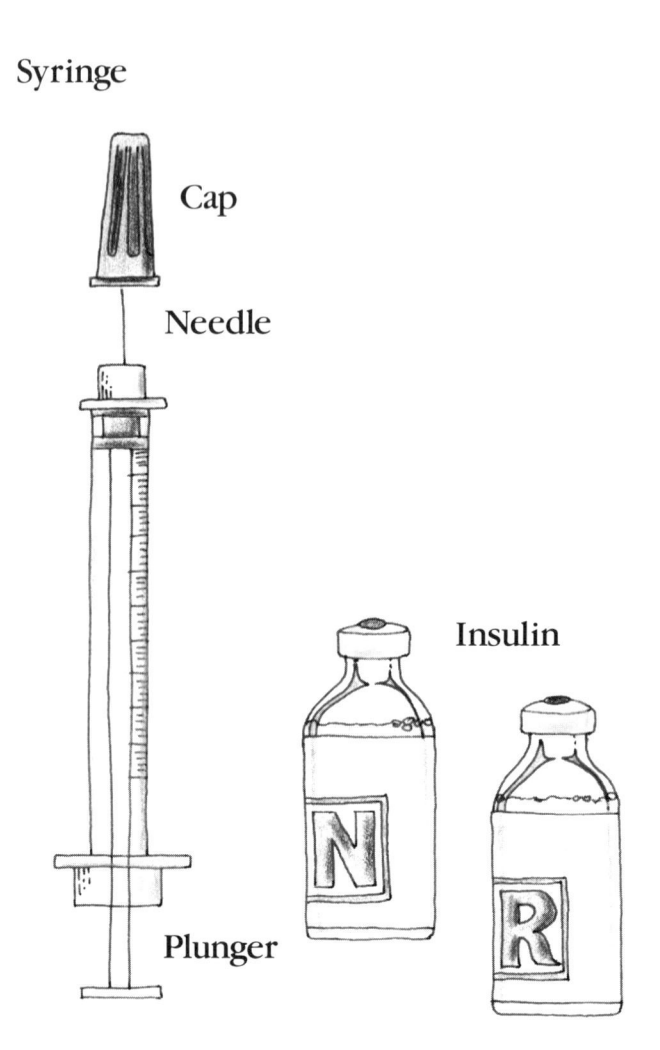

Syringe

Cap

Needle

Insulin

Plunger

2. Wash your hands.

3. Roll the cloudy bottle of insulin between your hands.

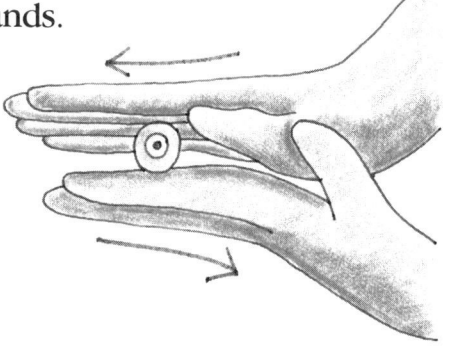

4. Take the cap off of the needle.

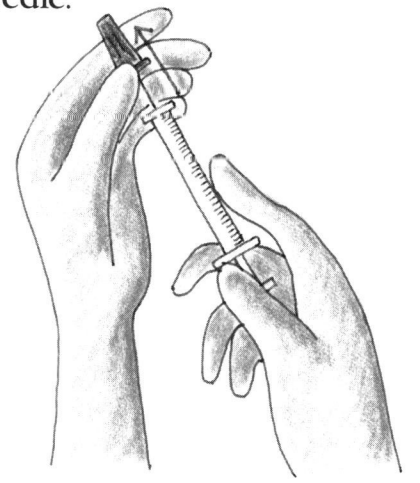

5. For the cloudy insulin, pull the plunger out to _____ units to let air into the syringe.

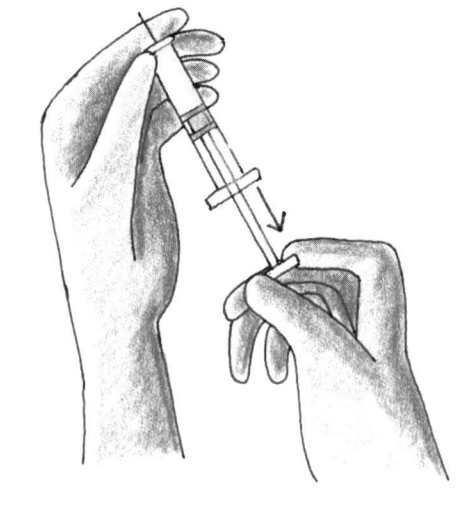

6. Put the needle into the cloudy bottle of insulin.

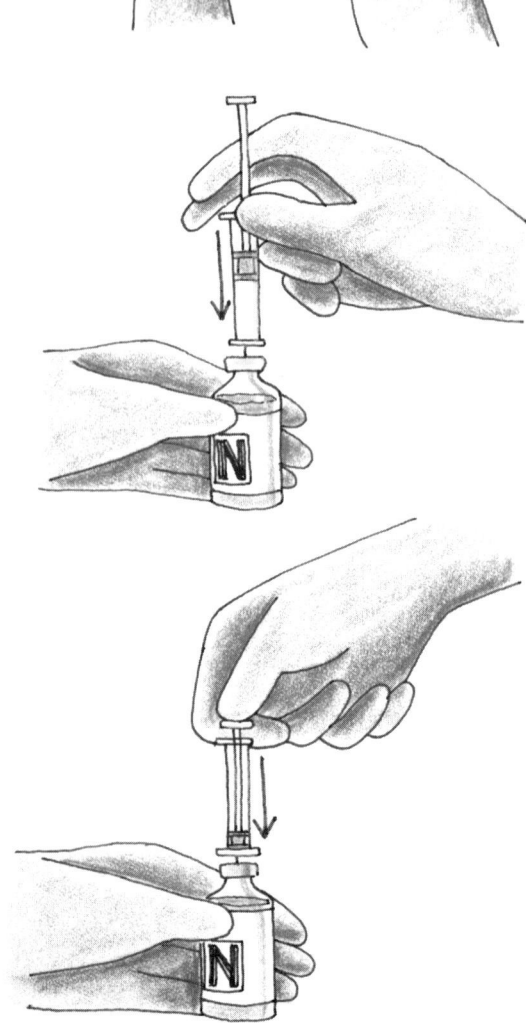

7. Push the plunger down. Shoot air into the bottle.

8. Take the needle out of the bottle.

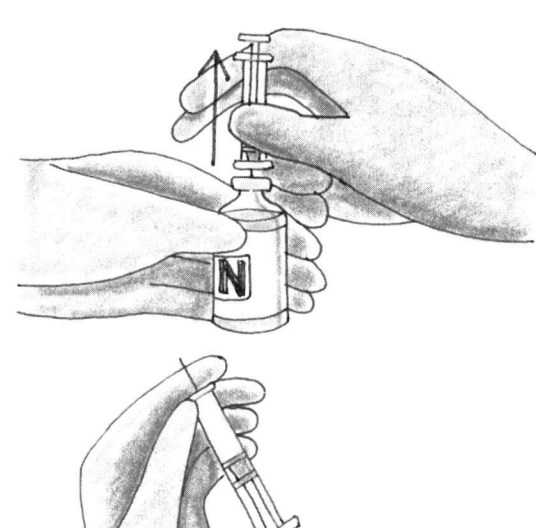

9. For the clear insulin, pull the plunger out to _____ units to let air into the syringe.

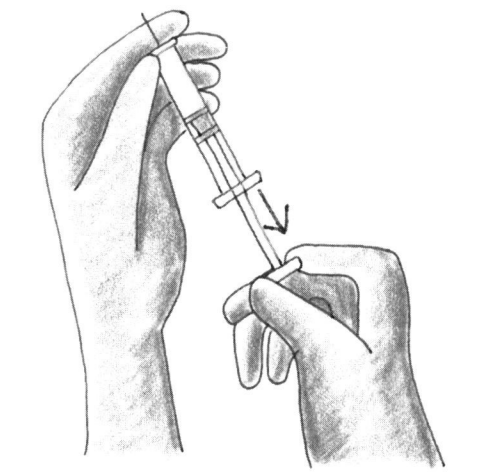

10. Put the needle into the clear bottle of insulin.

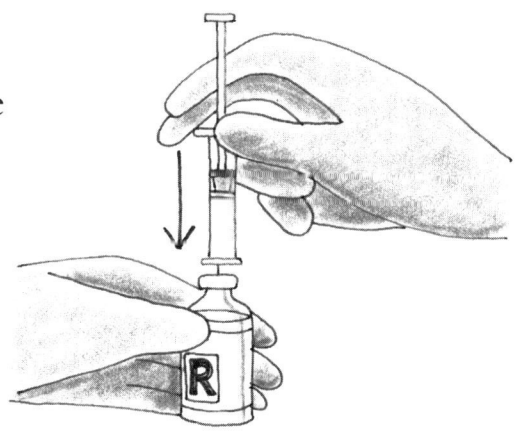

11. Push the plunger down. Shoot air into the bottle.

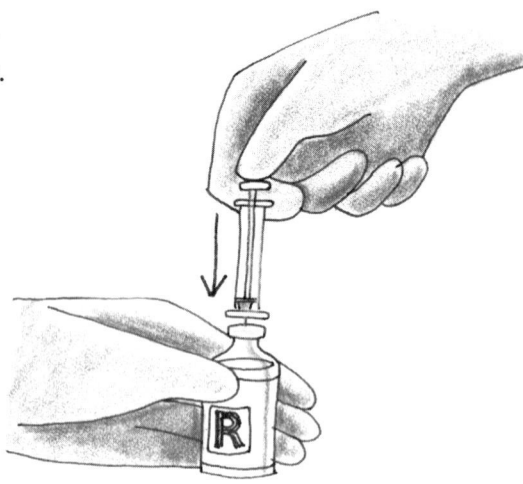

12. Turn the bottle of clear insulin upside down with the needle in it.

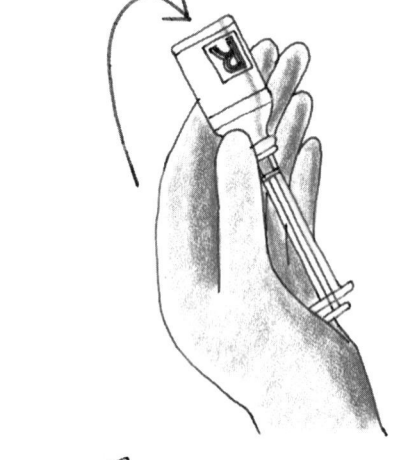

13. Pull the plunger past the amount that you take. Push the insulin back into the bottle. Do this two times.

    Pull the plunger out to _____ units of clear insulin.

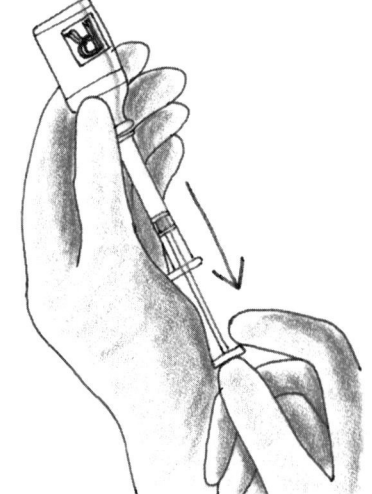

14. Check for air bubbles. (Air bubbles do not hurt you, but they mean you get less insulin.) If you have air bubbles, push the insulin back into the bottle and start from number 13.

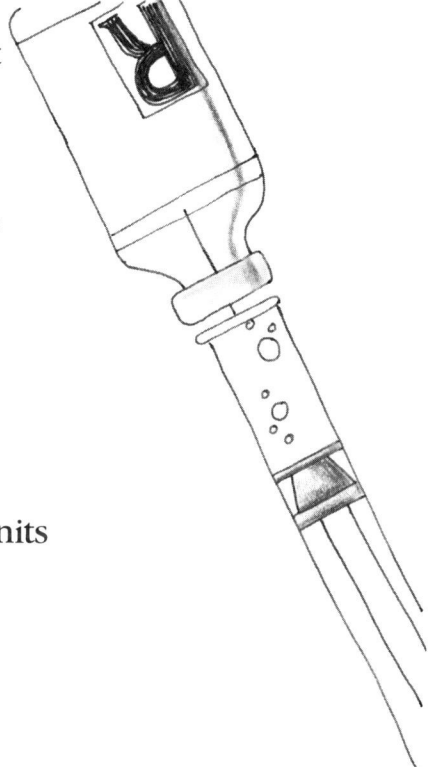

15. When you have _____ units of insulin in the syringe with no air bubbles, you can take the needle out of the bottle.

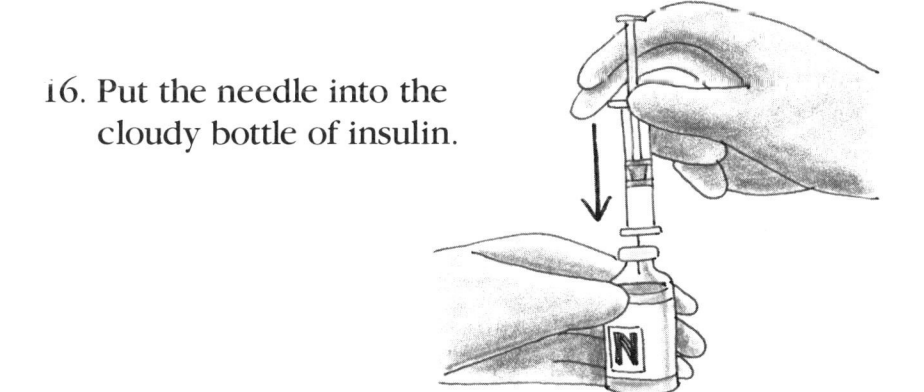

16. Put the needle into the cloudy bottle of insulin.

17. Turn the bottle of cloudy insulin upside down with the needle in it.

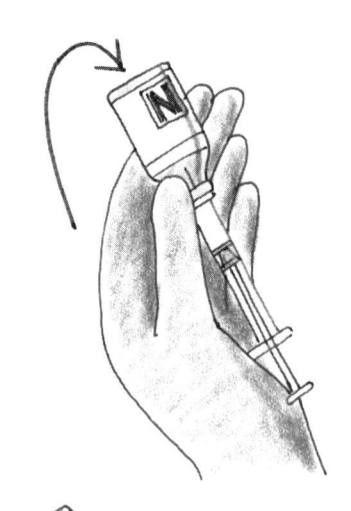

18. Carefully pull the plunger out to the <u>total</u> units of insulin you need.
    _____ units of clear
    + _____ units of cloudy
    = _____ <u>total units</u>.

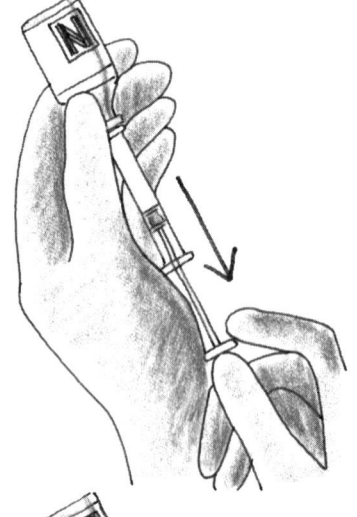

19. Take the needle out of the bottle of cloudy insulin.

20. Now you are ready to give your shot.

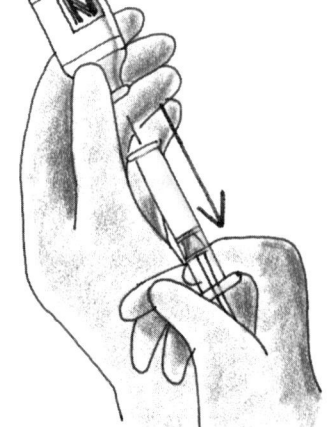

Give your insulin shot in a new place every day.

Give your shot this way:

Pinch up your skin.

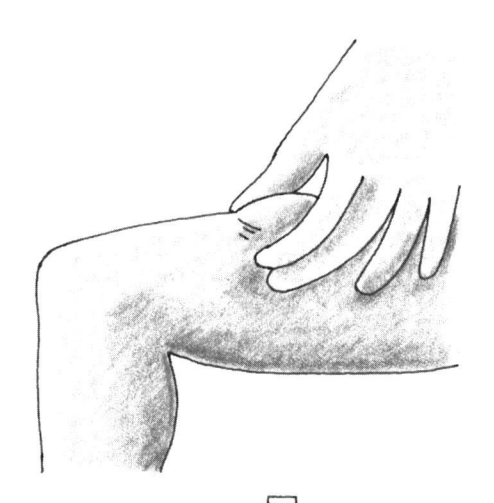

Push the needle through your skin.

Let go of the pinch.

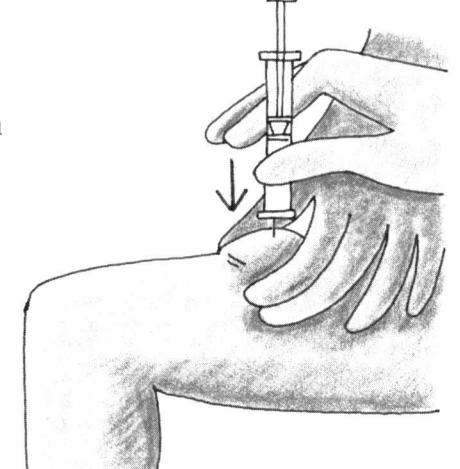

Push the plunger down.

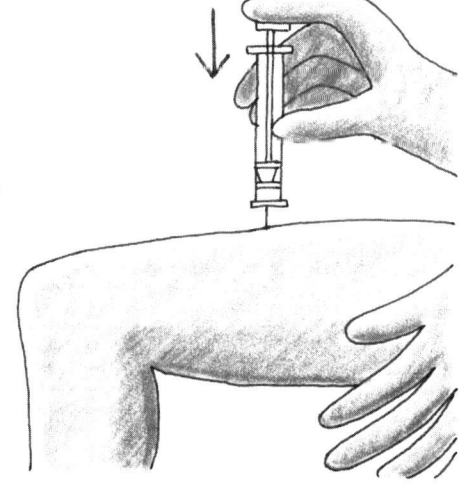

Take the needle out of your skin.

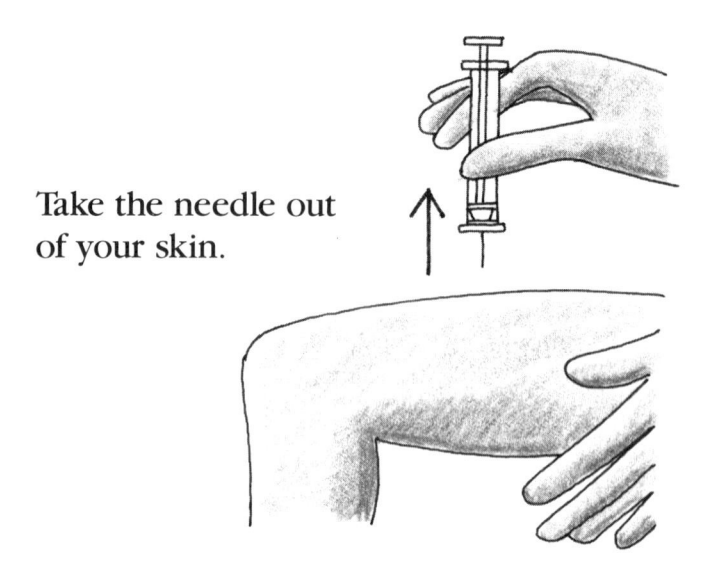

Put your finger over the place you gave your shot.

Take your insulin at

Exercise

Exercise

You will feel better if you exercise. Exercise can:

- Improve your health.

- Help you lose weight or stay at a good weight.

- Help lower your chances of getting heart disease.

- Help lower your blood pressure.

Exercise can help insulin work better in your body. This will help lower your blood sugar.

Things to do for fun and safe exercise:

Ask your doctor if there are any reasons why you should not exercise.

Choose an exercise that you will like.

Some good exercises are: walking, biking, swimming, jogging.

Walking

Biking

Swimming

Jogging

Wear shoes that fit your feet.

A good time to exercise is after a meal or snack.

Try to exercise at about the same time each day.

Exercise 4 to 5 days a week.

Start slow. Work up to:

> 5 minutes of warm-up: stretching or marching in place

> 20-30 minutes of exercise: walking, biking, swimming, jogging

> 5 minutes of cool-down: stretching or marching in place.

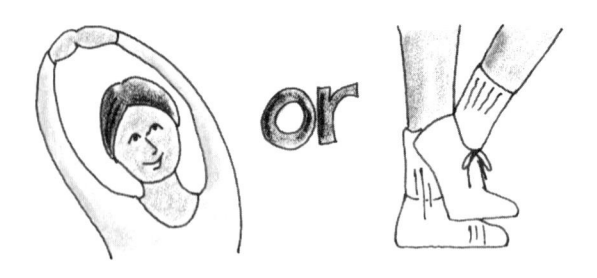

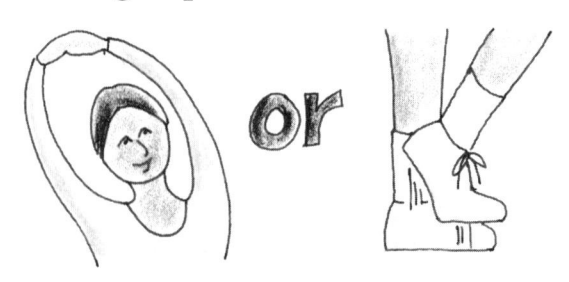

Stop exercise if you feel:

    pain in your chest

    pain in your legs or feet

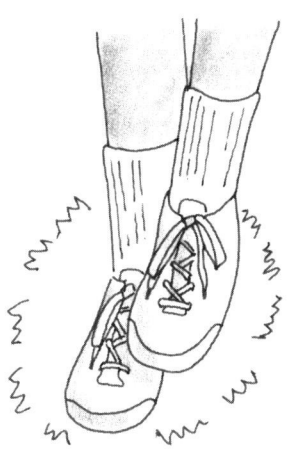

    out of breath.

    Have fun with exercise!

If you use insulin:

Remember the best time to exercise is after a meal or snack.

If you feel you are having a low blood sugar before or after you exercise, eat a snack such as

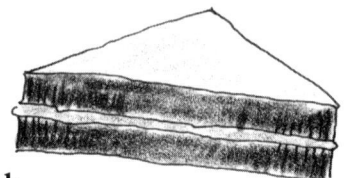

½ a sandwich,

or or or...

a piece of fruit,

or_____

Always carry some food with you when you exercise in case you have a low blood sugar. Some good foods to carry are:

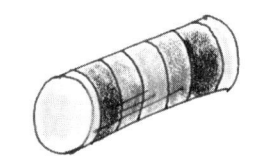

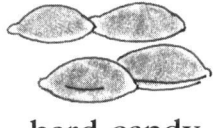

lifesavers

hard candy

a small box of raisins

or_____

If you use insulin and test you

Test your blood sugar before you exercise. You may need to i

If your blood sugar is:

Less than 100

If your blood sugar is:

Between 100 and 180

If your blood sugar is:

Between 180 and 300

If your blood sugar is:

More than 300

… blood sugar:

… the amount of food you eat for exercise.

… eat a snack such as:

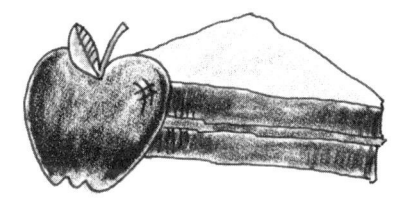

½ a sandwich and a piece of fruit

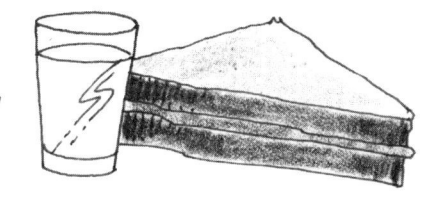

or ½ a sandwich and a glass of milk

or _____

eat:

or ／ or ◯ or …

a piece of fruit or _____

You do not need to eat an extra snack

Be aware – blood sugar may go higher.

Test your blood sugar during exercise that is longer than one hour.

If your blood sugar is less than 100, eat

 or or or...

a piece of fruit

or_____

Test your blood sugar after you exercise.

If your blood sugar is less than 100, eat

 or or or...

a piece of fruit

or_____

Remember:

Know what exercise does to your blood sugar.

Write your blood sugars in your record book.

Write the kind of exercise you did.

Write how long you exercise.

If you exercise with other people, tell them how they can help you if you have a low blood sugar.

You should always wear your diabetes bracelet or necklace when you exercise.

Low or High Blood Sugar

Low Blood Sugar

Low blood sugar is called hypoglycemia. Insulin reaction and insulin shock are other names for low blood sugar.

You may have a low blood sugar if:

- You have too much insulin or diabetes pills.
- You do not eat all of your meals or snacks.
- You do not eat your meals or snacks at the right time.
- You forget to eat your meals or snacks.
- You get more exercise than normal.

When you have a low blood sugar your body will tell you. You may feel:

shaky

sweaty

tired

hungry

dizzy

crabby

confused

You may also have:
blurry vision

headaches

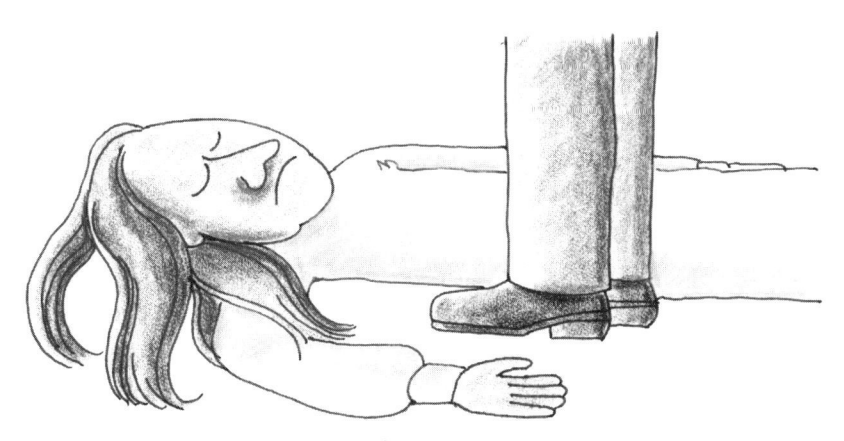

You could: pass out

If you feel this way, test your blood sugar. If the test is lower than 80 you need to eat something that will bring your blood sugar up fast.

If you feel this way and cannot do a blood test, you should eat something that will bring your blood sugar up fast.

Some foods you can eat are:

½ cup of fruit juice

1 small box of raisins

1 cup of milk

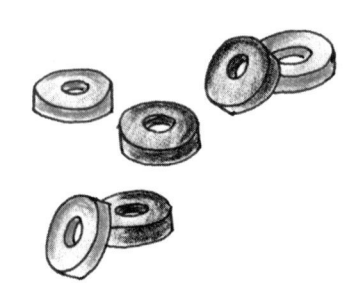

6 or 7 lifesavers

½ cup of regular soda pop

5 small sugar cubes

3-4 glucose tablets

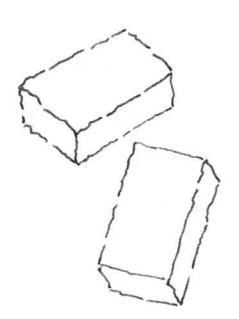

2 big sugar cubes

If you do not feel better in 10 to 15 minutes, eat the same amount of food again.

Remember:

Always carry some food with you that will help bring your blood sugar up fast.

Always wear your diabetes necklace or bracelet.

You can always get help when you need it.

− Tell your family and friends and people at work that you have diabetes.

− Tell them you may need help if you have a low blood sugar.

− Tell them some things they can do to help you.

Like:
- give you some juice or soda pop
- call 911 if they cannot wake you up
  or _____

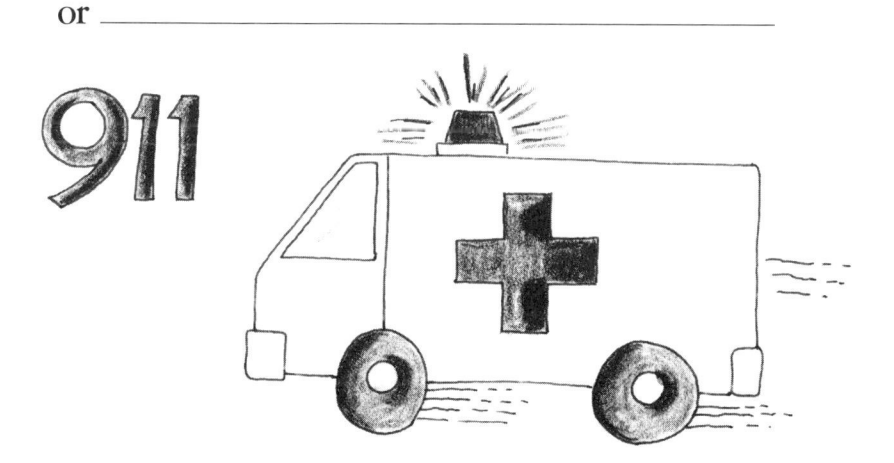

Your blood sugar is too low.

Why?

You forgot to eat your meal or snack.
You did not eat all of your meal or snack.
You did not eat your meal or snack at the right time.
You got more exercise than usual.
You took too many diabetes pills or you took too much insulin.

Your body will tell you.

You may feel:

shaky   dizzy
sweaty   crabby
hungry   confused
tired

You may also have:

blurry vision
headaches

You could pass out.

What to do:

1. Check your blood sugar.
2. Eat or drink something that will help your blood sugar go up fast.
3. Follow your diabetes plan.

High Blood Sugar and Ketoacidosis

If your blood sugar is too high, it's called hyperglycemia. Hyperglycemia can result in a dangerous problem called ketoacidosis. If ketoacidosis is not treated, you can become very sick or even die.

Too high a blood sugar happens when there is not enough insulin. This causes blood sugar to go up and stay too high. When this happens, it means your diabetes is out of control.

You may have too high a blood sugar if:

- you don't take enough insulin or diabetes pills.
- you are sick. A sore throat, vomiting, diarrhea, bad cold, or infections can all cause blood sugar to go up.
- you ate too much food.
- you have a lot of stress.

If your blood sugar is too high, then the body isn't getting enough sugar for energy. If the body can't use sugar for energy, it will use fat. When the body uses fat for energy, ketones are made. Ketones will get into the blood. Ketones in the blood may give you some of these problems:

You could have pain in your stomach.

You could vomit.

You might need to go to the bathroom a lot.

You could have fast breathing.

This problem is called ketoacidosis.

The body will try to get ketones out of your blood. The ketones will go into the urine. You will need to do a urine test for ketones if you are sick or your blood sugar is over 240.

If your blood sugar is over 240 mg/dl and you have ketones in your urine, call or see your doctor or nurse right away. Do not wait.

Test your urine for ketones:
1. When you are sick.
2. When your blood sugar is 240 mg/dl or higher.

Your blood sugar is too high.

Why?

You did not take enough insulin or diabetes pills.
You ate too much food.
You did not exercise.
You are sick.

Your body will tell you.

You could have pain in your stomach.
You could vomit.
You might need to go to the bathroom a lot.
You could have fast breathing.

What to do:

1. Check your blood sugar.
2. Check your urine for ketones.
3. Call your doctor or nurse when your blood sugar is over 240 and you have ketones in your urine.

Sick Days

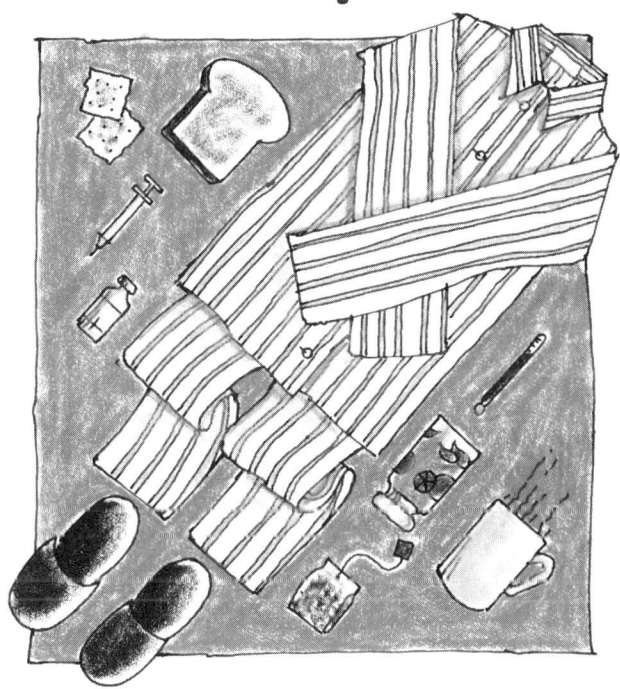

Sick Days

When you are sick your blood sugar may go up.

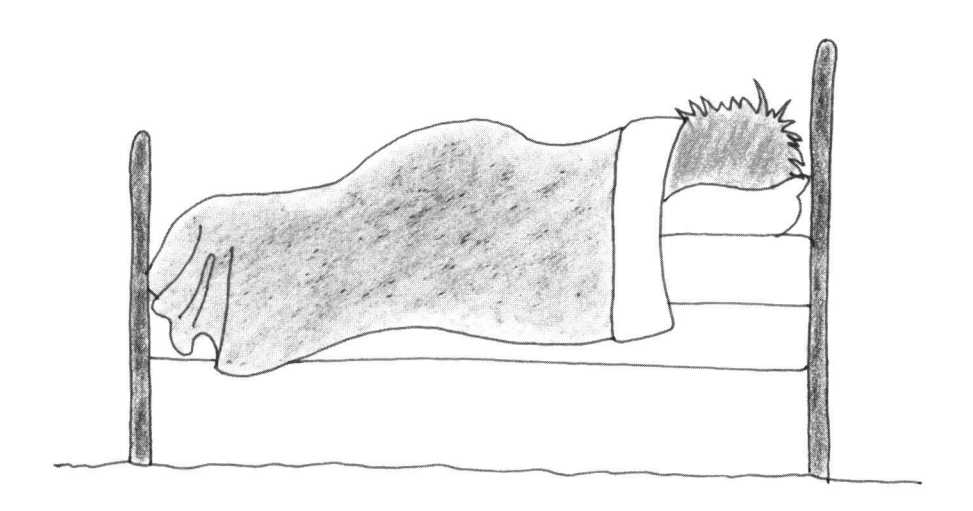

Here is what to do if you are sick for one day:

If you take insulin, take the same number of units of insulin you always do.

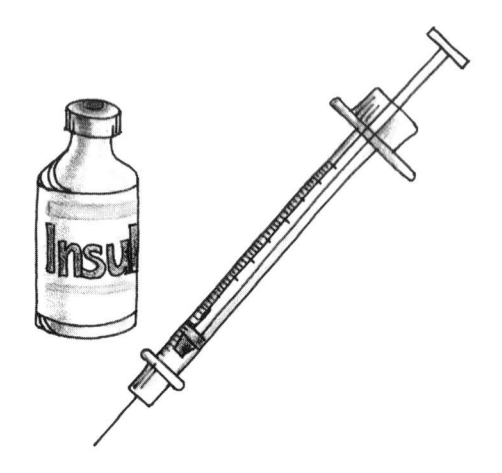

If you take a diabetes pill, take the same number of diabetes pills you always do.

If you vomit, do not take your diabetes pills until you can eat without vomiting.

If you vomit, take the same amount of insulin you always do.

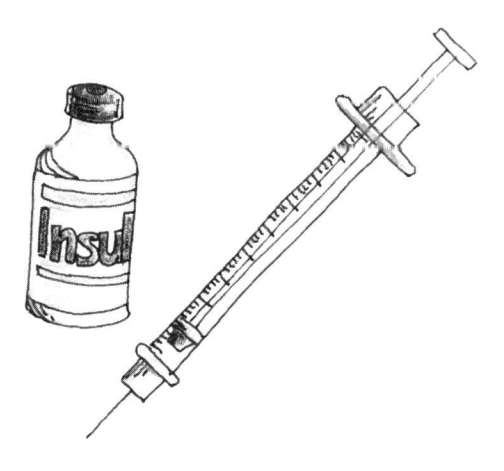

Test your blood sugar every 4 to 6 hours.

Test your urine for ketones every 4 to 6 hours.

Eat your usual meals and snacks.

and

131

If you cannot eat your usual meals and snacks, eat or drink or

Food		How much
regular soda pop	=	¾ cup
orange juice	=	½ cup
ice cream	=	½ cup

these foods slowly every 45 to 60 minutes.

Food		How much
sherbet	=	¼ cup
soup	=	1 cup
toast	=	1 slice
soda crackers	=	6 crackers

133

Also drink a lot of water, tea, and broth. Drink one large glass or cup full every hour.

When you feel you can eat again, eat a small snack. Then eat your usual meals and snacks at their normal times.

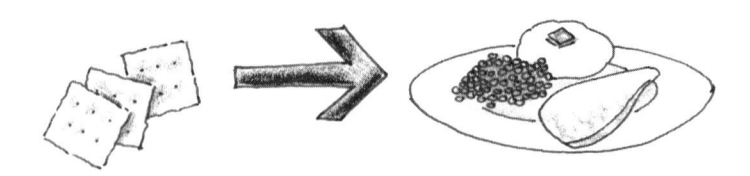

Call your doctor if:

You are sick for more than one day.

You vomit.

You cannot eat your usual meals and snacks for more than one day.

You have moderate or large ketones in your urine.

You have pain in your stomach.

You have diarrhea.

You have fast breathing.

Foot Care

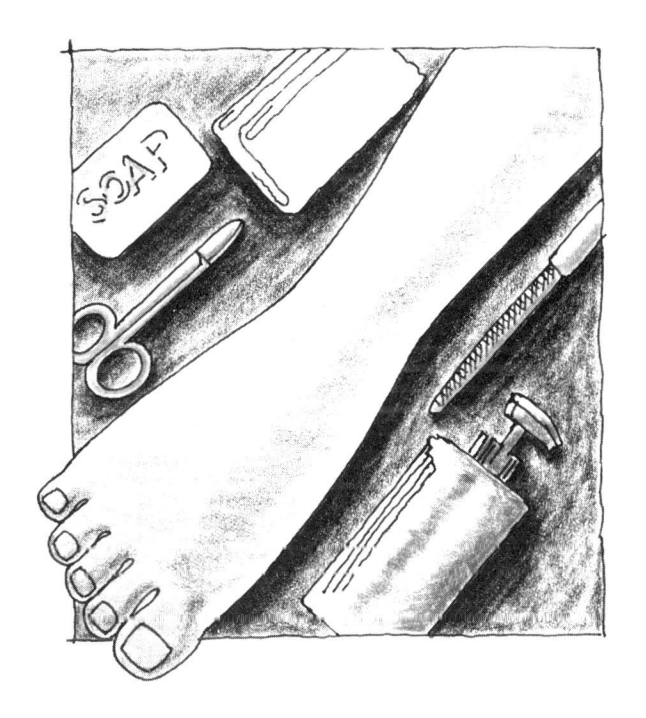

Foot Care

Diabetes can hurt the nerves in your feet. You may get "funny feelings" like "pins and needles" in your feet. Your feet may "go to sleep."

Diabetes makes blood vessels get old and hard faster. Then it is hard for your blood to get to your legs and feet. This is poor circulation.

You may have poor circulation if:

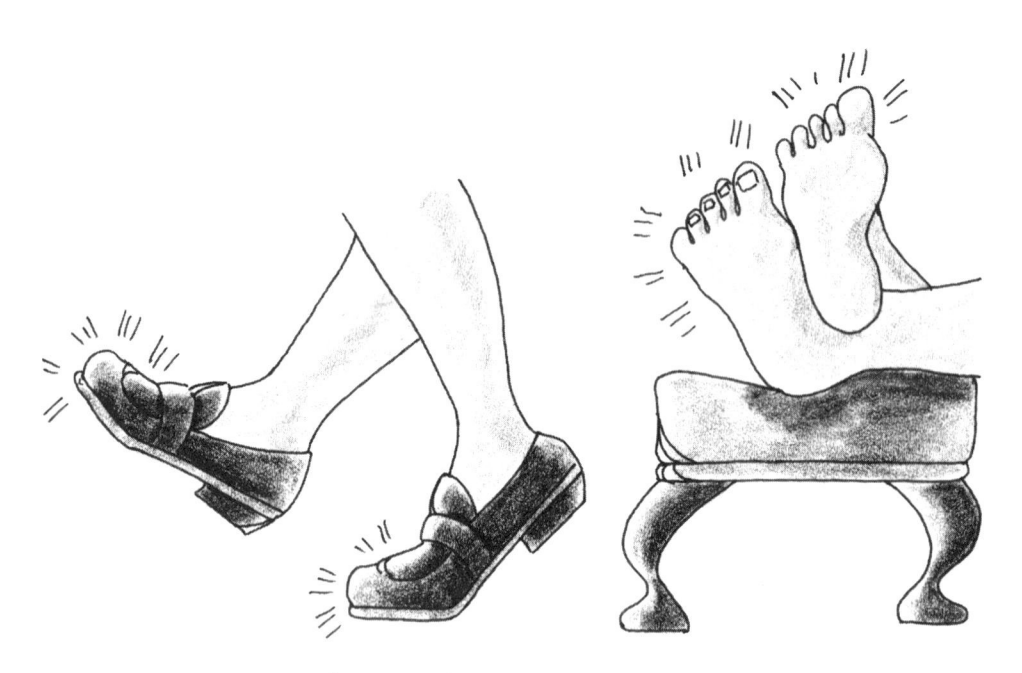

Your legs or feet hurt while walking or resting.

Your legs or feet hurt at night when you are sleeping.

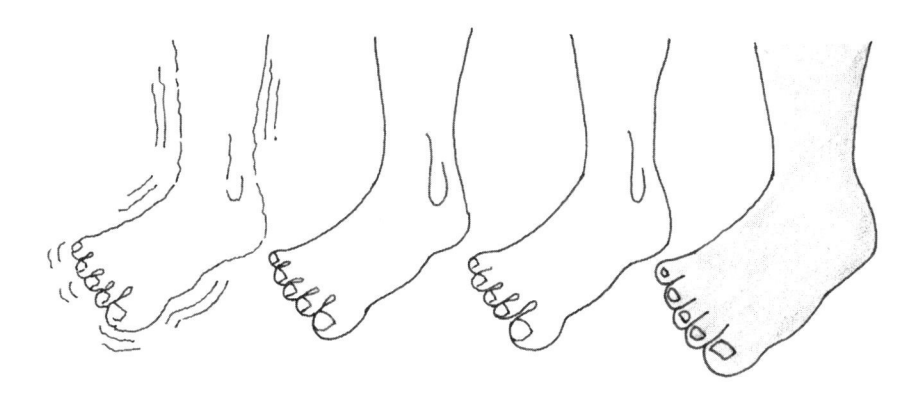

Your feet are cold, pale, blue, or puffy.

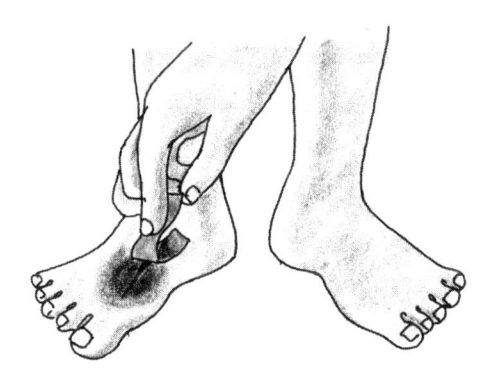

Your feet have cuts that don't heal.

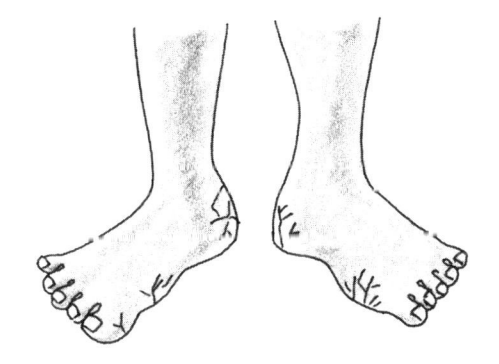

Your feet are dry and have cracks in the skin.

If you have any of these problems,
call your nurse or doctor.

There are things you can do to take care of your feet.

Do these things:

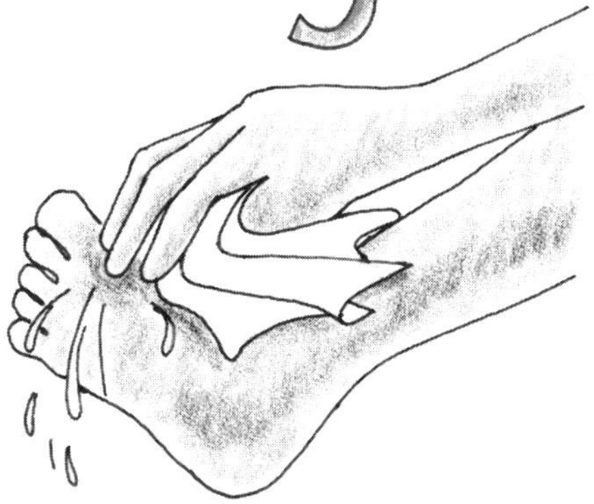

Wash your feet every day.

Use warm water and mild soap.

<u>Do Not</u>
<u>Use Hot Water</u>

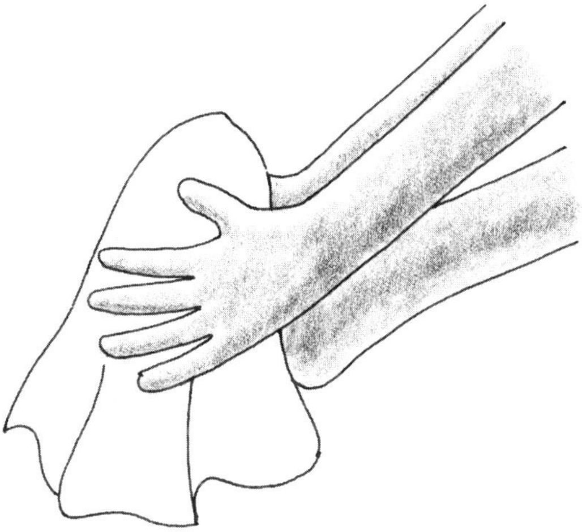

Dry your feet well. Also dry between your toes.

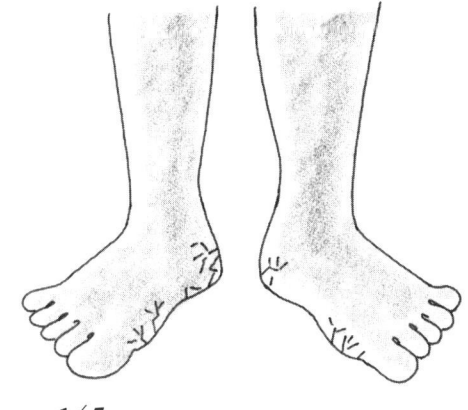

Look at your feet for cracks, dry skin, or cuts.

Do these things:

Use lotion to help keep the skin smooth.

Keep your toenails cut straight.

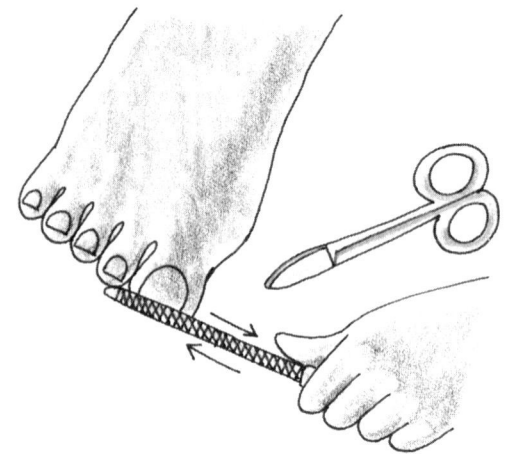

Wear shoes that fit your feet.

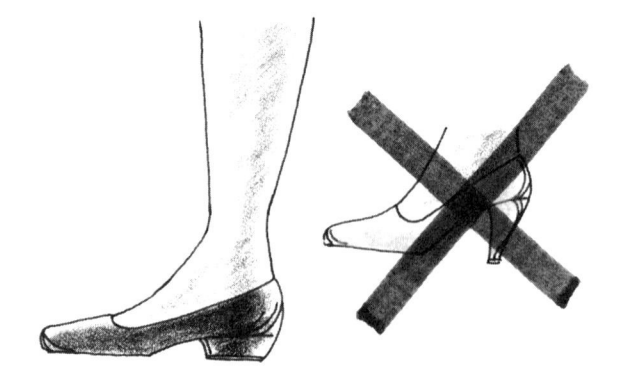

Do these things:

Look inside your shoes for any rocks or other things before you put them on your feet.

Wear clean socks. Cotton is best.

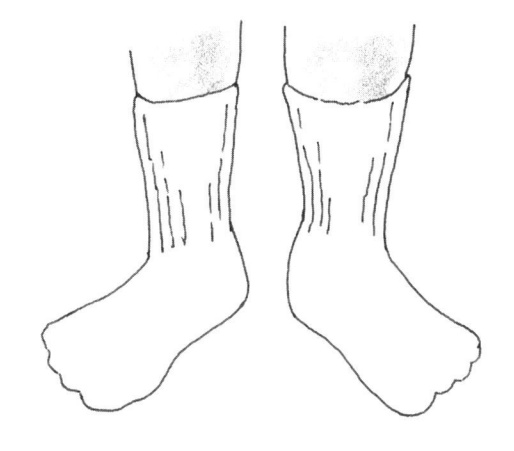

Call your nurse or doctor if you have any problems with your feet.

There are also things you should not do.

Don't do these things:

Don't soak your feet!

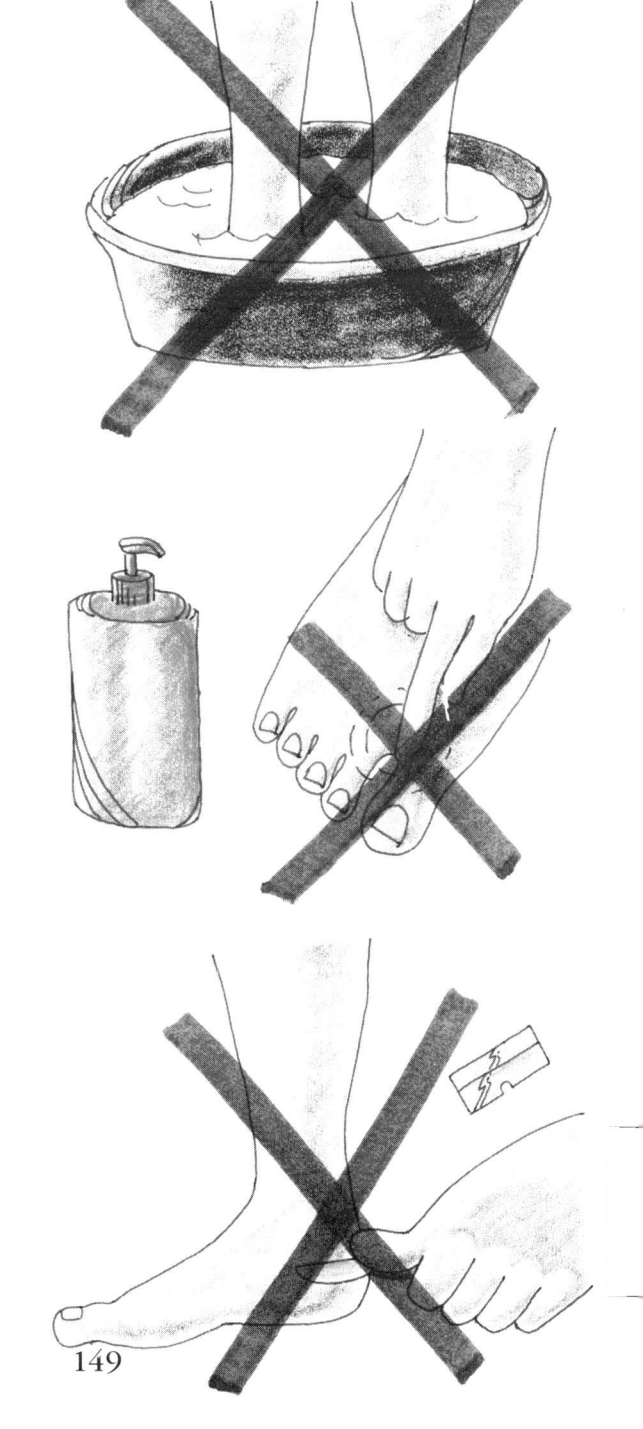

Don't put lotion between your toes or on cuts.

Don't use sharp things like knives or razor blades to cut skin on your feet.

Don't do these things:

Don't go barefoot.

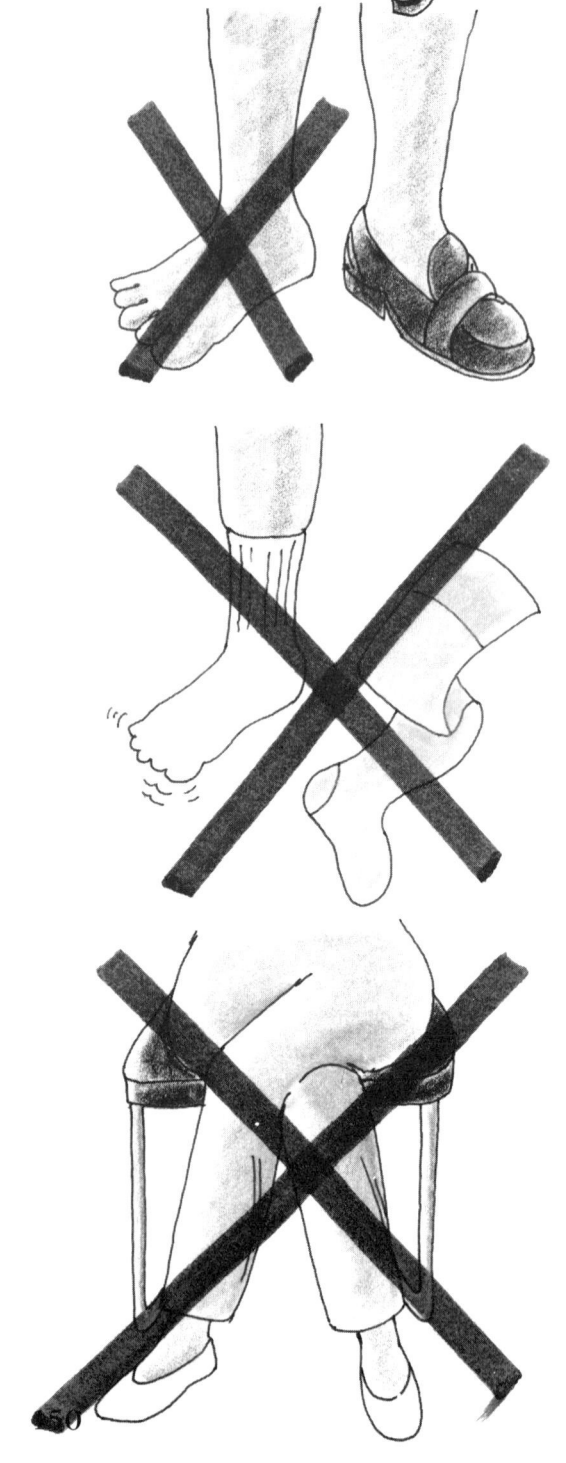

Don't wear tight socks, nylons, or garters.

Don't sit with your legs crossed.

Don't do these things:

Don't use heating pads on your feet.

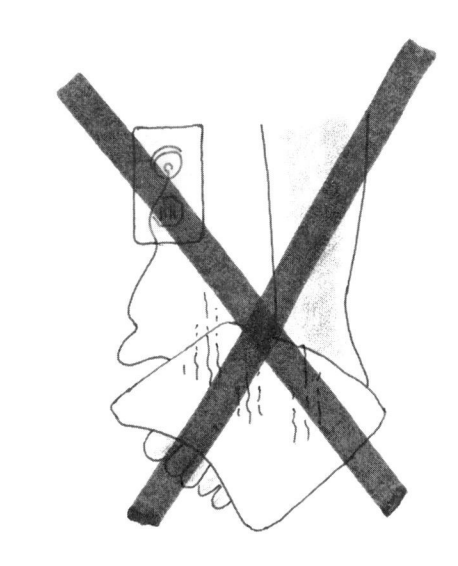

Don't walk if you have open sores or cuts on your feet.

Don't wait! Call
your doctor or nurse
if you have any
foot problems.

Always wear your
diabetes necklace
or bracelet.

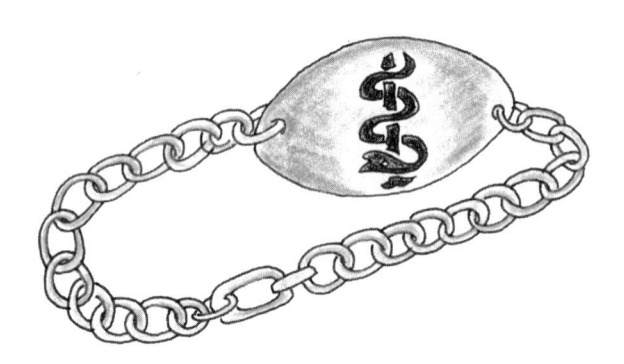

Hope for the Future.

Hope For The Future

Scientists are trying to find out who will get diabetes, better ways to treat diabetes, and a cure for diabetes.

The future for people who have diabetes is bright. But it is important for you to control your diabetes today so you can be helped by diabetes research tomorrow.

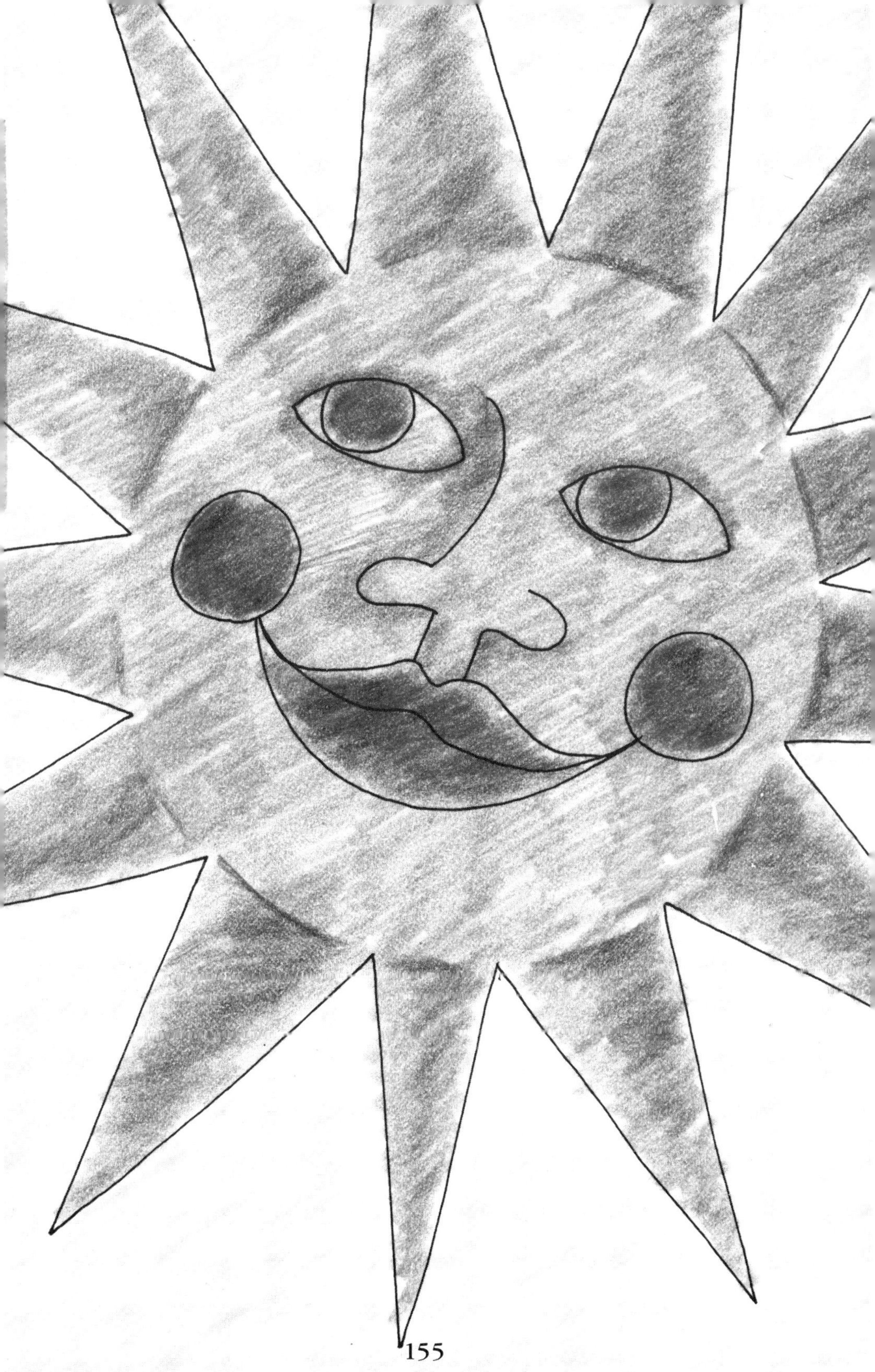

Hm 873-TN
25